AF326570

FINDING GOD

FINDING GOD

Discovering the Divine in the Gritty and Unexpected

LAURA HEIKES

Foreword by Darrell L. Whiteman

CASCADE *Books* · Eugene, Oregon

FINDING GOD
Discovering the Divine in the Gritty and Unexpected

Cascade Books
An Imprint of Wipf and Stock Publishers
199 W. 8th Ave., Suite 3
Eugene, OR 97401

www.wipfandstock.com

PAPERBACK ISBN: 978-1-6667-3129-3
HARDCOVER ISBN: 978-1-6667-2364-9
EBOOK ISBN: 978-1-6667-2365-6

Cataloguing-in-Publication data:

Names: Heikes, Laura.

Title: Finding God : discovering the divine in the gritty and unexpected / Laura Heikes.

Description: Eugene, OR : Cascade Books, 2023 | Includes bibliographical references.

Identifiers: ISBN 978-1-6667-3129-3 (paperback) | ISBN 978-1-6667-2364-9 (hardcover) | ISBN 978-1-6667-2365-6 (ebook)

Subjects: LCSH: Christian life—Meditations. | God (Christianity)—Omnipresence—Meditations.

Classification: BV4501.3 H44 2023 (print) | BV4501.3 H44 (ebook)

FEBRUARY 10, 2023 10:08 AM

For Kevin, Anna, Leah, and Asher . . . the ones I delight to come home to.

The whole universe and all events are sacred, serving as doorways to the divine for those who know how to see. . . . For those who have learned how to see fully, everything—absolutely everything—is "spiritual."

RICHARD ROHR

Contents

Foreword

Where in the world is God? John 1:18 reminds us, "No one has ever seen God." And yet, we know so much because of Jesus who lived among us. As followers of Jesus, we believe that God is everywhere, yet sometimes we cannot find him, as if he is hidden.

In the past thirty-five years many of us have been captivated by British illustrator Martin Handford's popular books *Where's Waldo*, which have sold over seventy-five million copies in twenty-two languages worldwide. Waldo, dressed in his red-and-white striped shirt and sporting a red-and-white cap, is sometimes hard to find, but we know he's there, hiding in plain sight, somewhere in the picture. Once we spot him, we can't miss him.

Pastor Laura Heikes, drawing on twenty years of leading Methodist congregations to know God, to love God, and to worship God, is going to take us on a "scavenger hunt," looking not for Waldo, but for God. Some of her stories will appear to be out-of-the-box behavior and we may wonder if this is proper pastoral demeanor, but then Jesus also "colored outside the lines" of the establishment and religious leaders of his day.

Today, some followers of Jesus believe that we can find God best in a daily quiet time. For others, God shows up in times of raucous, enthusiastic worship, or God appears in formal liturgical corporate worship. Some find God most clearly by reading the Bible, while some discover God in nature. Still others who try to do all the right "churchy things" end up empty-handed, wondering where in the world is God. Perhaps we're looking in the wrong places. Like Waldo, God may at first be hidden, until we attune our hearts, eyes, and ears to discover where God is already present. That's what Pastor Laura teaches us to do.

In the stories that follow you'll laugh, cry, and frequently be surprised at where Pastor Laura found God. Some places seem downright scandalous, but then again, Jesus scandalized the church people in his day too.

Although she's not an anthropologist like me, Pastor Laura has honed some very good listening and observational skills and she believes we can learn them too. As you read through these captivating stories of finding God, try out some of her suggestions at the end of each chapter. You'll learn some helpful tools for engaging the world in which we live and discovering God's presence there. Here are a few:

- Listen more and talk less.

- Pay attention and avoid distraction.

- Focus on making careful observations and "see" what is unseen or "hear" what is unsaid.

- Look especially outside the four walls of the church—Augustine is reputed to have said that God has many the church doesn't have, and the church has some that God doesn't have.

- Develop sensitivity for the little interior nudges from the Holy Spirit.

This book will take you on an exciting journey, finding God in some very unusual places as well as in the mundane, everyday events of life. We'll look at the world differently when we do. We'll be able to move beyond our comfort zone and into what I call a learning zone (but still short of the dreaded panic zone). Over time, as you look for God in unexpected places, your learning zone will feel more and more comfortable. You will discover that you no longer fear getting out of your comfort zone because you know you will encounter God, who has already been present in the lives of the people and communities you engage, long before you get there.

The following chapters are organized along the lines of the instructions that Jesus gave to his disciples just before he ascended into heaven. He empowered them to be faithful witnesses in Jerusalem, Judea, Samaria and to the ends of the earth. As disciples of Christ, we are also called to be witnesses in our home community (Jerusalem), in the region of the country where we live (Judea), among those people we would rather avoid (Samaria), and yes, even among people and communities around the world (the ends of earth). Wherever we go, Jesus promised to be there with us, and we'll discover that God got there before we did.

Darrell Whiteman
Gig Harbor, Washington
May 2022

Acknowledgments

In my second year of ministry my colleague, Larry Howard, suggested that we preach a shared sermon series about finding God outside the walls of the church. He looked for God in the hospital and on the fishing pier. I gravitated toward the rodeo, an unemployment line, and a bar where folks danced in cages. Though we visited different places, we both enjoyed the search. This experience was so profound that I continued the practice in every church I've served over the past twenty years. I'm grateful to Larry for nearly two decades of friendship and for his wonderful idea, which was the seed of this book.

Another seed came from my former professor, Darrell Whiteman. Sitting in Darrell's class, I felt as if the separate threads of my faith were suddenly pulled together to reveal a beautiful pattern for ministry. I discovered how my love of people and culture fit beautifully with my love of God and the Bible.

As this book came together, Judy, Merrijo, and Rosemary read through the manuscript for me. Their careful eyes caught typos mine had slid right past.

This book couldn't have happened without the wonderful folks in the four congregations I've led. You gave me ideas, taught me about your communities, went with me even when it worried you, and helped others discover God in places nobody thought to look before. I love you. Life is better with such a wonderful family of believers at my side.

And speaking of family—mine is the light of my life. I'm so thankful to have people I can return to after all these adventures. Of all the places I have met God in this life, my favorite is in our family.

Introduction

My favorite class in seminary was taught by a professor in a suit and tie . . . and Birkenstocks! Twenty years ago, Dr. Whiteman's suit and sandals ensemble created quite the buzz. But what I remember about his class, all these years later, is that sitting there I felt years of searching come together—how we served a God who loves us so much, he became *one of us*. And how we, following in Jesus' steps, should know not just our Bibles, but the terrain of our communities: the history, the culture, the traditions, the felt needs. Many good pastors get to know their churches. But how many pastors spend the same care getting to know their neighborhoods?

Dr. Whiteman urged us to spend time in the restaurants, bars, and parks around our churches. Believers were called, he said, to share good news with the entire community. And no matter where we went, God had already beaten us there. Dr. Whiteman pointed over and over to Acts 14:16–17: "In the past [God] permitted all the nations to go their own ways, but he never left them without evidence of himself and his goodness. For instance, he sends you rain and good crops and gives you food and joyful hearts."

There is evidence of God *everywhere*. Everywhere! This means you and I can approach the divine not only in worship, or on Sunday morning, or in a quiet prayer time, but throughout our lives. We can meet God while waiting in line for groceries. God can speak to us as we take out the trash. God can encourage us as we wait for the bus. There is evidence of God *everywhere*. We just need to learn a new rhythm, the spiritual practice of keeping our hearts, our eyes, our ears open to God throughout our days.

Acts 14:17 promises us something like a spiritual scavenger hunt. The "clues" are not impossible to find—God *wants* to be found by you and me. The signs are there for all to see. Long ago, magi (who had never read the Torah) saw a birth announcement in the stars. They came, they followed, they found their king and knelt before him. Witnesses to God aren't just churchy stuff, like an image of a dove in the water on the sidewalk. It might just as easily be your neighbor's discarded furniture.

The other day, on a morning walk, I came across just such a sign from God. There, on the side of the road, was the jankiest, most beat-up recliner I've ever seen. Its pleather surface was cracked and peeling. The recliner's cup holders were stained and sticky with years of spilled drinks. It looked frightful, like you might catch something just by stepping too close to it. A cardboard sign was propped on the worn seat: "Free!"

"No kidding," I thought. And also, "good luck," because nobody will look at that beat-up old recliner and see anything but trash. I was about to go by when I felt a little interior nudge that I have come to realize is the pull of God.

Weird. I stopped, backed up, and looked once more at the janky old recliner. And then I saw it—a witness to God. Because none of us put our good furniture on the curb, free for the taking. We place things on the curb only when they are used up and devalued, broken and unworking. Only when we don't want them anymore.

God did the opposite. God gave us the very best. God gave us the most beloved thing God had—Jesus. In my mind's eye, I suddenly could see Jesus, holding a little cardboard "Free!" sign, right there on the curb. Jesus, whole and perfect, powerful and loving, offering all of humanity grace, healing, forgiveness, and homecoming . . . for free. With Jesus, the good stuff is finally out on the curb. Free to all.

So, take a second look. Witnesses to God show up in broken furniture, at stop lights, in the grocery store. These clues are symbols that anyone can read, and they are all around us. Throughout this world are signs from God. Signs that point the way home. But only if we slow down, pay attention, and expect to meet God throughout our lives.

This is easier said than done. Most of us grow up learning to meet God in practices like worship, prayer, Bible study, and service. These lovely spiritual disciplines nourish and sustain us. But they all share something in common: they instruct us to set time apart, go someplace special or quiet, and retreat from the world to meet God. Church on Sunday with other believers, a quiet prayer time in a secluded corner of our homes, a small group that meets for coffee and Bible study—all these practices teach us to carve out time, wake up early, close our doors. We've learned to *separate* ourselves from the world to *connect* with God.

Don't get me wrong; this side of our spiritual lives is amazing, and fulfilling, and meaningful. We can spend a lifetime learning how to quiet ourselves enough to really listen, to really hear God. Worship, study, prayer: they fill and guide us; they shape and change and transform us. We could, and should, spend our lives growing and deepening these spiritual practices. But there is more, my friends.

This book is about the other side of spirituality—that of engagement. This book is an invitation to meet God in the world. To get curious about where God is outside the church walls and what God is up to. This is a book about how we meet God not only in separation from the world, but also in engagement with it.

Jesus models a rhythm of separation and community, of noisy crowds and quiet meals with his disciples. Jesus lives out a pattern of purposeful separation and passionate engagement. Jesus expects to meet God in times of quiet prayer *and* in the middle of a jostling crowd. Jesus isn't surprised when God's power is suddenly visible in a storm or at a tax collector's booth. Jesus teaches and heals in worship on the Sabbath *and* on dusty roadsides. And faith? He finds it, not just in crowds of the faithful, but also in the heart of a down-and-out Samaritan woman at a well, and in a Roman centurion, and in a healed leper.

The early believers followed Jesus' pattern of retreat and engagement. They separated themselves for prayer, worship, and the Lord's Supper. They also passionately engaged with their communities, counting on God to show up in the world around them.

There's a great example of this from Paul's time in Athens (Acts 17:17–34). Paul preaches in the synagogue to the Jewish believers and the God-fearing gentiles, and *also* spends time in the public square, speaking to the crowds (17:17) and debating some of the town's philosophers (17:18), which gets everybody talking. Paul quotes a local poet (17:28), compliments the people on their practice of faith (17:22), and even uses a pagan altar to point to God (17:23).

Paul can quote Scripture like nobody's business, and often does so when talking to Jewish believers. But when speaking to gentiles, Paul searches for touchpoints, places where God's presence is visible in their daily lives. In Athens, Paul walks through the town, noticing what the people are interested in. Athens is really into idols. They have a ton. Seeing this,

Paul realizes they are "very religious" (his words!—17:22). He then uses one of their altars, the one dedicated "To an Unknown God," to talk to them about the God they worship without knowing (17:23). A councilman and many others come to faith!

What might you see if you walked through your own town, neighborhood, or community, looking for how God is speaking? Because God is already at work in your town! And all that is missing is someone who can notice and point it out.

Throughout my ministry, I've been looking for God, both in times of separation from the world and engagement with it. This book is about the latter, about looking for signs of God's love out in the world, among ordinary people, in places we never thought to look. To organize this journey, I've drawn on Jesus' final words to his disciples: "You will be my witnesses, telling people about me everywhere—in Jerusalem, throughout Judea, in Samaria, and to the ends of the earth" (Acts 1:8).

Jesus' final words send his disciples out. To Jerusalem, Judea, Samaria, and to the ends of the earth. In the chapters that follow, we'll move outward in rings. The disciples, though not originally from Jerusalem, soon make it their home base. The Jerusalem section invites us to look for God in the ordinary spaces of daily life: getting a bite to eat, waiting in line, attending a football game.

When Jesus calls the disciples to Judea, it means leaving the comfort of home and venturing further afield. Judea is a stretch and a sacrifice, still manageable, but not fully "comfortable." In the Judea section, we'll look for God in places that are a ring or two outside our comfort zones: at the town dump, with a teenage driver, or attempting axe-throwing.

The final section, Samaria, invites us to go to those who, though geographically close, are culturally or religiously distant. Looking for God in "Samaria" invites us to interact with people who might live right next door, but whom we'd rather avoid: people downtown at midnight, those dancing in cages at a sketchy nightclub, the ones who party loudly and rambunctiously in a trashy place dubbed "Devil's Cove." Sometimes, the "Samaritans" in our life are geographically close but culturally, economically, politically, socially, even morally different.

Your rings of interaction, your Jerusalem, Judea, and Samaria, are probably different from mine. I might find myself at home in places that feel foreign to you, and you may be a native in places that feel remote and difficult for me. But we all have a Jerusalem, a spot where life typically takes place, and a Judea, where Jesus calls us beyond our comfort zone, and a Samaria, where we are called far beyond our borders to interact with people we'd rather avoid.

We go out into the world, farther and farther, because Jesus calls us. And we go with the hope and the expectation that God has already beaten us there; that there is no place in this world where God isn't already present; where there isn't already a witness, a sign, of God's love, if we only have the eyes and heart to see it.

The pages to come contain stories and reflections from two decades of searching. People in four different cities have walked with me among drunks and the diseased, through every place from RV bathrooms to middle school lunchrooms. I'd ask them where they'd least expect to meet God; then we'd go there, looking.

I've searched for God at Walmart, a livestock auction, and a demolition derby. I've been in roadside bars where men urinate in the parking lot and nightclubs where women danced in cages. I've visited a tattoo parlor where I sat across from a man with a loaded gun. I've been invited into the "Asshole Section" at a juke joint and allowed myself to be arrested and booked in jail. And never, not once, has God been absent.

Come with me. Meet God in unexpected venues. You will look at the world differently. And like Paul and Barnabas, you will be able to tell the people you meet that God is already with them; they just hadn't realized it.

Our first stop is "Jerusalem," that space of the world around you that feels most comfortable and known, but where you may never have expected to encounter God.

JERUSALEM
Noticing God in Your Daily Routine

1

Nutty Brown

Finding God on the Dance Floor

And forgive us our sins, as we have forgiven those who sin against us.

MATTHEW 6:12

I found God at a honky-tonk. Or maybe I should say, God found me and my family. The Nutt is a restaurant and music venue in the hills outside of Austin, and that night it was packed. Crowds filled the plastic chairs and tables that surrounded the outdoor stage. The Eggmen, an exceptional Beatles cover band, headlined. Their set has two acts: Early Years, with the band in matching blue suits and skinny ties, and Later Years, with neon Sgt. Pepper outfits. As the night wore on, the crowd began to sing, then dance along, filling the creaky wooden dance floor under ancient oak trees. As the sun set, washing everything in warmth, I saw God. At first, all I could do was sit and stare. Then my husband pulled out his phone to take a picture because the scene was miraculous, and one wants to remember such moments.

If you look at the picture we took, the place where we saw God, you might be confused. It shows two older women, dancing. One is tall, one is short. They are looking at each other, smiling. It's miraculous because these women have each been married to the same man. The first, the shorter one, met him when she was fourteen. He played tennis and she was on the dance team. They dated through high school, put each other through college, studied late for the bar exam and the CPA exam. They had three children together, took turns walking the floor on sleepless nights to let the other one rest. It got rocky. The third baby had just been born when the husband asked for a divorce. The first woman, at twenty-eight, became a single mother of three.

The second became a mother to three kids at age thirty-five, when she married that father. In an instant, she not only had a new husband, but step-kids ages nine, seven, and five. The two women loved the same kids, but they loathed each other. Mostly, they managed icy disregard (for the sake of the children). They celebrated major holidays separately, allowing the children to run from their car to the other's home, but not going in themselves. Not for years, not for decades, not when the children had grown and began to have children of their own. Even then, the hatred lingered.

Every week, for most of my life, I've said the Lord's Prayer with a group of believers. I began, as a child, saying it in a traditional church with an organ, a robed choir, and a pulpit we thought might double as a spaceship. In college, I prayed Jesus' prayer in an auditorium filled with students, lifting our hands in worship. I've served downtown first churches and new church starts. And this prayer, in the very same form, is like a thread through it all. Every week, in every one of those churches, I have asked God to forgive me my trespasses . . . and to help me to forgive those who trespass against me.

Trespass is an old word that means "wrongful entry on real property." In Texas, we are serious about not trespassing on someone else's land, and there are ways to mark private property. "No Trespassing" signs, of course. And barbed wire (we love barbed wire). But there's another way: purple paint. If you are hiking and encounter a band of purple paint, you know you've come upon private property. That paint barks out a warning—this is mine and you are not welcome here!

But how do you mark off your heart? How do you make sure no one trespasses there?

The heart is the most tender, private space you have. You can go to work, function in society, even get through rush hour traffic while mostly keeping your heart safe. We open our hearts at our own choosing, to people whom we trust to take care of them, to value us and tread lightly. But sometimes that trust is broken; someone we invited inside brings destruction and pain to those most vulnerable spaces. Instead of care, they walk with cleats, they kick things over, they break into private spaces. It hurts. A deep, throbbing wound.

When someone trespasses in your heart, you long to do the same to them. But Jesus' response is different. Jesus teaches that when people trespass, enter the heart without permission, and bring destruction, we should . . . forgive.

Mercy to criminals!? Forgiveness for those who have dragged mud across our hearts!? Grace for those who are clearly in the wrong!?

Yes.

It's hard. But yes. Each week, believers around the world give voice to the Lord's prayer; we use the words Jesus gave us. We ask God to forgive us.

But sometimes mercy and sincere forgiveness just take time. The deeper the pain, the longer the healing can seem to take. For the two women dancing at the Nutty Brown Café, forgiveness began with a baby. The first grandchild was born, and the women, together at the hospital, went to dinner to celebrate. The rest of the family watched nervously, barely eating, but neither woman threw flatware. Conversation, for the first time, remained warm.

For Thanksgiving later that year, the great-grandparents invited the family over to their house for dinner, as usual. But for the first time, *everyone* came. The grown children placed themselves between parents, living buffers, but no conflict arose.

The next Thanksgiving, they tried it again. And the women, mother and stepmother, found themselves doing dishes together. Even their children were starting to trust that they could be alone together. Elbow-deep in sudsy water, the mother took a deep breath and told the stepmother she was sorry for the hurtful things she'd done.

There was a long pause. For the first time in twenty-five years, the pain between them had been named, out loud. The mother waited. The stepmother stared back at her.

When the grown children entered the kitchen with the next round of dirty plates, there the two mothers were, arms wrapped around each other, crying.

So it was that three generations gathered under the oak trees of a little Texas honky-tonk one summer evening. One mother said to the other, let's go dance. And they did.

I happened to be there to see it. I knew it was a miracle because that's my mom, and that's my stepmom, who after twenty-five years showed us what it meant to forgive another's trespasses. And how sweet it could truly be.

Try This

- Whom do you need to forgive? Spend some quiet time thinking about this question. As names surface, write them down. Give yourself time and space, and write down any name that comes to mind. Then forgive them. If you need a guide, use this prayer: I forgive __________ for __________, which made me feel __________, and I release him/her to you, Lord Jesus.

- From whom do you need to seek forgiveness? If you are struggling to find the words, you might use this template as a pattern: I'm sorry for __________. It was wrong because __________. In the future I will __________. Please forgive me.

2

Tacos Veracruz

Meeting God at a Food Truck

For the hearts of these people are hardened,
and their ears cannot hear,
and they have closed their eyes—
so their eyes cannot see,
and their ears cannot hear,
and their hearts cannot understand,
and they cannot turn to me
and let me heal them.

MATTHEW 13:15

BUSY? STRESSED? FEEL LIKE you don't have enough time for all that happens in your day? Me too.

I wasn't looking for a prophetic word about stress and busyness when I visited the Tacos Veracruz food truck in South Austin. I was looking for breakfast tacos.

Tacos are one of the deep joys of my life, so when a member of my church suggested that I look for God at a food truck, I jumped at the chance to visit this bellwether. Tacos Veracruz is über-famous but attempts to shrug it off. Heck, the place only has ten parking spaces, which were, of course, taken. My friends and I drove into the little neighborhood nearby and parked along the street with all the other taco-hopefuls. It was a Thursday morning in July, which, if you don't live in Texas, means it was already ninety degrees at 9 a.m. At a food trailer, you sit outside. I felt like a sweaty, melting mess. A frumpy one at that.

But the diners at nearby picnic tables could have been in a magazine representing the cool Austin vibe. There was a guy on a one-wheel scooter with a big chunky tire. I think he had a dog . . . wait, of *course* he had a dog! It's *Austin!* There were men with braids; women with amazing sleeve tattoos. Everyone drew, sketched, or wrote dialogue lines for their new indie film in moleskin notebooks. And the footwear! I spent ten minutes trying to read one guy's shoes. Everyone there likely spent hundreds of dollars to look like they shopped at a thrift store.

Then came the tacos. And suddenly, I forgot that I was an uncool, middle-aged mom, and simply enjoyed. The flavors were so good. It was worth melting in the summer heat surrounded by hipsters if these were my last bites of sustenance.

As we ate and looked for God, my friend Amber quietly pointed out a couple behind us, whispering that they'd been to the counter three times. It wasn't a problem with their order. They just hadn't yet gotten the perfect picture of themselves. They came back to get a better angle, a cuter candid-looking shot. I glanced at them throughout our time and always saw them with their phones up, snapping pictures of themselves, their meals, themselves *with* their meals. When they weren't taking pictures, they stared at their phones. They'd look up every so often to eat bites or add salsa.

They were there, like us, to experience the best breakfast tacos in the nation. And this was likely their first time at Tacos Veracruz because they were so carefully documenting it. But I'm not sure they even *tasted* the tacos! They were so distracted.

As I watched that couple, God spoke a challenging prophetic message to me about the little device I carry everywhere. The thing I never leave home without. My cell phone.

After the food truck, I started noticing how much time *I* spent with my phone. And I worried that, like the couple, this device was causing me to miss out on deeper experiences. One morning, as I prayed, I felt God urge me to check my usage.

On first glance, I felt good. I mean, the Bible app was right there at the top. And then texting—which, I told myself, is mostly work and family. But then the next one on the list: 42. That's a domino game. Kevin and I used to play 42 in college. It takes four people, and you play with partners and bid on hands. I was never that good. But then—some utter genius developed an app that lets you hone your skills without needing three other people! That week, I'd spent 3.2 hours playing my domino game. That's almost thirty minutes a day, playing dominoes.

I knew I liked it, but where in my hugely busy schedule had I found thirty minutes each day to play a domino game? I'm sure it was while I waited for the kids to get out of school . . . or maybe before bed? A small, difficult voice reminded me: there were times I was sitting on the couch, staring at my phone, playing dominoes while my kids or my husband tried to engage me in conversation.

If I had to choose family or dominoes, I'd say family! And if you asked if I have enough time with them, I'd tell you "no." But friends, if I gave up dominoes, I'd have thirty more minutes every day with my family.

Is it just me? Or do all of us need to find God at the food truck? Let's grab a breakfast taco and get real with the way our phones are robbing us blind. It might be social media, it might be email, it might be sports or fantasy leagues, online games, or online shopping. Maybe you're one of the rare people who isn't developing a crick in your neck from looking down at your phone. But I bet there's *something* that steals your time and your focus. Something that shifts your priorities without your consent. Something that distracts you from spending time with God.

Where did I see God at the food truck? In the prophetic call to lay those things down and focus on God and the truly good things in this life.

In the Scripture that begins this chapter, Jesus warns that many of us will be blind and deaf to what really matters. We can have eyes but be unable to see; ears, but still not hear the most important voices:

"Come play with me, Mama."

"Let me tell you about my day."

There is so much good in our lives: our homes, our kids, that delicious taco. But do we take the time to really see it?

Every generation reads this verse and grapples with the ways they are tempted to turn off their ears, eyes, and hearts. At the taco stand, I saw ours. We carry it with us in our pockets, every single place we go.

Of course, phones are very good. They help us do work. They can make emergency calls and connect us when we're far apart. Phones provide information, news, music, and even turn-by-turn directions. Phones can even enable family time; because of cell phones, I don't have to sit at the office waiting for a phone call. Because of cell phones, I can video chat with my grandma and study the Bible with friends around the nation.

But . . . phones are also a temptation. One of the most wonderful inventions can also block your ability to see your life, connect with those you love, and experience the world around you.

Let's take it a little further. Could it be that your phone is hindering your spiritual life? Stealing time you might have with fellow Christians—or with God? I do not want to lay burdens on you. We all need time to unwind. We all get bored. And sometimes, having a phone can help you get something important done. But it can also chain you to the wrong things.

Almost all of us would agree we are busy. We are so, so busy that we feel stretched to the limit.

But are we?

Are we really?

Or is our time going to the wrong places?

I found God at a food truck when God pointed out a temptation, a thief of time, a place where being an "average American" isn't spiritually healthy.

When we intentionally take a break from our phones, we'll be amazed at all the places we see God in this world, and the people who have been right next to us all along.

Try This

- If you have a smartphone, take a deep breath and check your usage. How many hours do you spend each day looking at that phone? Which apps take the most of your time? How do you feel as you confront your use of time? What would "ideal" look like? If you decrease your screen time, what will that give you more time to do? Where will you invest your regained time?

- Choose one night a week to fast from screens. List out fun activities you enjoy that don't involve technology, and do those things on your screen-free night. If you have a family, involve them.

- Ponder the notifications you receive on your phone. You can change all of them! Resolve to turn off all but the most vital notifications so that you are more in control of your time and your screen usage.

3

Kneeling on the Goal Line

God in High School Football

I focus on this one thing: Forgetting the past and looking forward to what lies ahead, I press on to reach the end of the race and receive the heavenly prize for which God, through Christ Jesus, is calling us.

PHILIPPIANS 3:13B–14

MAYBE YOU'VE HEARD ABOUT high school football in Texas?

Perhaps you saw *Friday Night Lights*?

It's true—we take football very seriously in Texas.

I was born and raised in Texas (San Antonio, if you were wondering), so it took a long time (and moving out of state for a few years) for me to realize that, in other parts of the country, not everyone is into high school football. Even in Texas, the larger the town is, the less impact high school football has on the community. Everybody enjoys it, sure, but we don't all go to the games. However, get out of the big cities, and that town's team, or teams, are a source of civic pride.

I spent a decade in one such place. Now hold your horses . . . it's not the stereotypical small Texas town you might be imagining. First off, it's on the south shore of beautiful Lake Travis, which is just outside of über-cool Austin. The population in that area exploded about fifteen years ago: great schools, better land prices, and a gorgeous lake. Tons of people decided to make a thirty-minute commute into Austin for the sake of living outside the city snarl. Little fishing cottages from the sixties now share lakefront space with million-dollar mansions.

But everybody, whether they're driving a pickup or a Tesla, is rooting for the same team. No, not the Longhorns, although, yes, them too. I'm talking about the Lake Travis Cavaliers. Everyone, whether they have school-aged kids or not, has Lake Travis (LT) apparel (they sell it at the grocery store, so there's really no excuse). Most folks also have an LT sticker on their car (whether they have a student or not). On every shirt, jacket, hat, and koozie is a star for every year we have won state (that would be six, if you're interested).

Did you catch the pronoun? A star for every year *we* have won state. First person plural. *We* won state. I do not play on the team. I don't have kids who play on the team. Still, when the Cavaliers win, it's a win for *me*. A win for *us*. A win for the whole dang community. *We*, the people of Lake Travis, have won! *We* have been victorious over our enemies (the people in *other* communities). Some of them really are jerks, I swear. (More on that in a minute.)

Sometimes, though, being a fan is a real chore. Football gets started in August, which is the hottest, most awful time of the year in Texas. In August, you inevitably begin to wonder why in the world you live in this inferno of a state. Some summers are okay, others are scorchers. When the asphalt starts to get a little squishy under your feet, you know it's bad. I remember a summer when I crossed the street and felt it sink a bit. I knew without even seeing a bank thermometer—we'd reached the next ring of hell. That particular summer, Texas experienced sixty-one straight days of 100+ degree temperatures. It was on one of those afternoons, when the temperature soared to a record 112 degrees, that Cavalier football kicked off.

We were playing Westlake (gross), a town just to the north who thinks equally poorly of us. They had printed up shirts which proclaimed, "Westlake is the *Best* Lake."

Ahem.

To clarify . . . at that point, Westlake hadn't beaten us in *years*. But Westlake is the "old money" school in the area. They think Lake Travis is full of trashy lake rats. We think they are unbearable snobs.

It's a huge rivalry. Both teams compete for state championships each year. The rivalry, name recognition, and caliber of the teams led the University of Texas (UT) to invite us to play the season opener at Darrell K.

Royal Memorial Stadium, home of Texas Longhorn football. Expectations, already high, reached a fever pitch. TV crews set up cameras as fans searched for parking and made their way to the stadium. By the time we walked the half-mile from where we'd parked, we were soaked with sweat. But nobody wanted to miss this game!

The news got worse when we entered the stadium. Lake Travis was the visitor, so our fans sat on the "sunny" side. Which meant we felt like we were on. The. Sun.

Sweat rolled down my spine and sides. Cold water sold for seven dollars a bottle and it felt like a bargain, even though you had to drink it before it evaporated. I counted the seconds until the sun went down and glared at the Westlake fans, who were smugly reclining in the shade.

And there, in the middle of that overwhelming heat, I got an unexpected glimpse of God. As our team took the field, they went—as one—to the goal line, and knelt to pray.

All along the length of the goal line, each player found a spot and took a knee. For some, it was tradition. For others, just a ritual. For still others, a time to pray. But whatever their reasons, each player knelt there quietly on the wide line that marked the end zone. It touched me.

The team would spend the next two hours struggling to get back to that white line. They would use all their strength, wisdom, and training to push against a foe equally determined to keep them away. They would work together, execute plays to move them forward, respond to setbacks, capitalize on opportunities. But they began by kneeling in the place they wanted to end up.

As they knelt on the goal line, I saw God.

On a very basic level, it's important to know where you're going. Which isn't as easy as it sounds. At some point, I bet you've gotten in your car to go somewhere and been miles down the road when you suddenly realized—you're going the wrong way! Your brain, on autopilot, was dutifully taking you to work or to school, the places you drive without thinking, day after day. That well-worn path is like muscle memory, you find yourself just making the turns by habit.

Accidently finding our lives on autopilot doesn't only happen when we're driving. We can go through the motions in life without stopping to ask the most important question: Where do I want to end up?

Many of us are asked to come up with goals at work, or to abide by those of our supervisors. Lots of us have small goals for each day, our to-do list. Maybe we even set goals at the beginning of each new year (which most of us have abandoned by February).

I wonder—in the most important event, the living of your life—do you know where you are going? Or are you running hard without a clear idea of where the finish line even is?

What *is* the goal line of your life? If you are a Christian, you might say: "To live a life that pleases God." All people want our lives to have purpose, meaning, impact that goes beyond us. But *how* we live a life pleasing to God, how we make a difference, will look different for each of us.

What about you? What's the goal line? What will reaching the end zone look like? What is it you want to accomplish, overcome, or set right? What steps do you need to take to get there? Without a plan, a goal is nothing more than a penny tossed into a fountain.

Sometimes it helps to take big questions in pieces. You might start with the central relationships in your life. If you are married, what is God's desire for your marriage? I'd suspect it's more than just hitting fifty years, renting a limo, and having a nice dinner. God would like to see you give and receive support, encouragement, passion, and love. God would like your marriage to be like a garden where you can find rest, refreshment, and peace (Song 4:12–16).

If you have children, what goal line do you hope to reach with them? Many parents will admit they are on autopilot just to get the kids up, dressed, and to school with all their books, projects, sports equipment, and food. They work a full day, then come home and work a different full day: homework assistance, dinner, evening activities, then grab as much sleep as they can before starting all over. Kneeling on a goal line beyond surviving this week can feel impossible.

But ask yourself: Why did God give you these specific children? So you can enjoy them, first of all. Children, as the Bible says, are a gift from God to us (Ps 127:3). And looking at all of Scripture, it seems they are ours so we can teach and lead them, get them ready for life, and give them the character tools they need to thrive. Ask yourself: What do you want your kids to know, to have learned, to be part of their character before the year is up? What tools, resources, and character strengths do you want to instill in them before they drive away to college? Find the goal line, kneel there, and ask God to help you use the time you have with them to reach it.

What about work? For some of us, our working hours are primarily a way to support ourselves and those who count on us. But all of us can work for the Lord (Col 3:23). What goal line is there in your job? How could you use those forty to sixty hours, not just to earn a living, but to add to your life, to touch a need in the world?

How we live a life that pleases God is different for each of us. We share the long-range goal—a life that pleases God—but the hash marks are unique. Where is God calling you in the next few months? What does faithfulness look like this month, this year, in this town, in this church, in this stage? Think that through, and you'll know the goal line. Once you do, you'll have an idea of the steps along the way!

This is your life. Look around—this job, these relationships, this city, these friends. It's not tidy, it's not predictable, but it's yours. And the best way to not end up with handfuls of regrets is to meet God at the goal line and pray for help, every day.

Vince Young is beloved in Austin because he played for the Longhorns. With him as quarterback, UT won a national championship. Young went pro and had a career that didn't live up to most people's expectations. But there are a couple of shining moments. One of those is when his team, the Titans, played the Arizona Cardinals.

The Titans were down seventeen to thirteen at the end of the game. Young gets the ball on his own one-yard line with two minutes and thirty-seven seconds remaining. This is bad. For you non-football folks out there, he's got to take his team across the entire field, or ninety-nine yards of it, in two-and-a-half minutes to win.

In those final minutes, the Titans have an eighteen-play drive. Not every snap is successful. Young's sacked once, throws some incomplete passes, and completes a few for only small gains. Seconds leak away each time. But Vince Young doesn't give up. If a play fails, he focuses on the next snap, the next chance to advance the ball. And the Titans make it. Not in one Hail-Mary play, but in eighteen plays that take them ninety-nine yards in two minutes and thirty-seven seconds.

If you find a clip of that drive, you'll hear the announcers explain the victory like this: Vince was "keeping his eyes down the field."

That's what we can do too. Paul says it like this: "I focus on this one thing: Forgetting the past and looking forward to what lies ahead, I press on to reach the end of the race and receive the heavenly prize for which God, through Christ Jesus, is calling us" (Phil 3:13–14). Kneel on the goal line to seek God's help. Put your eyes on the end of the race and let that guide your steps.

The goal—a life that pleases God. A life that has purpose, relationships with meaning and growth. Ask God for help, for clarity about how you can reach that goal line, then run the plays. Don't get discouraged. Like Vince Young, like all good football players, just keep your eyes down the field.

Try This

- Find a soccer field, baseball diamond, track, football field, or any other place with a goal of some kind. Sit on home plate, in the goal box, or on the line that represents victory. Ponder all the steps it takes to get there. What must be done prior to the game? For how long? What must happen on the day of the game? What if it rains or one player is sick? How many people are involved in victory: players, coaches, trainers, support staff? Now ponder: What one or two goals does God have for you this week? This year? Ask God to help you see how you'll get there and be with you as you move forward. Ask God to put a team around you. Pray for each goal as you sit in that place. Pray for God to help you reach it in your life.

- Go to a cemetery. Wander through the rows of tombstones. Read the inscriptions. Try to picture the people who are buried there. Imagine having your life boiled down to a sentence or two. Consider—what do you want your sentences to say? Sit by a tombstone and talk to God about the ultimate goal of your life. Ask for God's guidance in moving forward with purpose.

4

"No, don't stare . . ."

Meeting God at the Bus Stop

Keep on asking, and you will receive what you ask for. Keep on seeking, and you will find. Keep on knocking, and the door will be opened to you.

LUKE 11:9B

THE CHURCH I LED in Spicewood, Texas, sits on a hill overlooking Lake Travis. In the spring, families bring their little ones to take pictures in the fields of bluebonnets that blanket the church grounds. Deer bed down among the trees. We've had a roadrunner, a wren, some mice, and even a stray dog in our sanctuary at various points. It's weird. And lovely. And remote. The nearest grocery store is twenty-five minutes away. So was my kids' school.

The first bell at Bee Cave Elementary rang at 7:45 a.m., which meant the bus stopped in our neighborhood out in the "sticks" at 6:30 a.m. It didn't come to our house, mind you. It stopped at our neighbor's home, up the hill, about half a mile away if we walked, much longer by car. Every morning, we'd walk up from our house to the end of the road, cut across the eighth hole of Willie Nelson's Cutt-N-Putt golf course, push through an empty lot, and finish in our friend's driveway.

But I'm making it sound so tame. Often, a wild scramble struck at 6:20 a.m. "Let's go! We gotta hustle!" I would shout, taking off up the hill with whichever child was ready. The slower one could then finish whatever last

18

task was delaying her and run to catch us. "We'll hold the bus," we'd yell back over our shoulders to the tardy sibling as we raced toward the bus stop.

Every now and then, though, we'd arrive with plenty of time to spare. On one of those rare, wonderful mornings, I saw the most embarrassing thing. Heard it, really. We all did. A woman stood in the shadows of a doorway across the street at 6:20 a.m., banging unabashedly on a darkened door. The sky, the street, the house in question, were all dark. The unlucky man who lived in the house across the way was a musician who often played gigs until the early hours of the morning. He rarely stirred before midday. Did I mention it was 6:20? *a.m.*?

Peering into the gloom while trying to appear as if I *wasn't* staring, I thought I recognized the woman making the racket. Wasn't that the neighbor from the log home down the street? I didn't know her name, only that she and her husband zipped around in a bright yellow golf cart. It was also becoming abundantly clear that this unknown neighbor was tenacious. She wasn't giving up or getting tired. She just kept banging on the musician's door, insistent and impossibly loud, in the early morning stillness.

What could be going on? My mind tried to find a plausible explanation. Was she expected? Did the musician need a ride to the airport? Was she also his wake-up call? Were they supposed to go somewhere together? Maybe she needed help? No . . . surely she didn't need *general* help, because there were two families standing at the bus stop right across the street, trying not to stare as she kept on knocking and hollering. If she had needed help, she could have asked us. *Would* have asked us. This was clearly a woman who had no problem being direct.

When the banging had gone on for a full minute, one of my girls asked in her not-so-quiet-kid-voice, "Mom, what is that lady doing?" I shushed her, told her I had no idea, but not to stare.

Then we all went back to pretending not to look while trying to watch out of the corner of our eyes.

Ask yourself this question:

How long would you be willing to knock on someone's door
> in the dark,
>> with an audience,
>>> if they didn't answer?

And what could possibly be so important that you would keep at it even when it became obvious you *weren't* wanted?

As I stood on that dark street, trying *not* to look, I felt God draw my eyes back. "Watch this," God whispered. "You, who live and breathe in a culture that saves face, you who never leave home in your robe, you who answer 'Fine' whenever someone asks you how you are, watch this person lay it *all* on the line. This," God said, "is what it's like to pray."

Would you like to know how to pray? How to *really* pray? How to pray the way some folks do, with power and faith? That's what Jesus' disciples wanted. As the disciples watched Jesus, a question, a longing, grew in their hearts: "Teach us to pray" (Luke 11:1). *Please*, the disciples ask, *Jesus, teach us to pray like you do.*

Power flowed through Jesus' life. Power the likes of which the disciples had never experienced, never seen before. Jesus was busy, but never stressed. Homeless, but never in need. Tired, but never "burned out." Prayer precedes Jesus' big decisions, prayer closes Jesus' days, prayer opens Jesus' mornings.

Jesus prays following times of intense work. Jesus prays to bring healing. Jesus prays to find the way. *Teach us*, the disciples beg. *Teach us how to pray like you do.* In response, Jesus gives them the words we call the Lord's Prayer. But then he goes on, explaining who can pray (everyone!) and illustrating it with a story: the story of two neighbors and a midnight request.

Prayer, Jesus says, is like standing on God's doorstep, knocking. But the verb tense indicates continuous action, "keep on knocking." This is not one polite tap on the door. No, the pray-er in Jesus' story is banging and banging on the door, throwing caution to the wind (just like the woman across the street from us at the bus stop).

Looking at her, I wonder if I could ever do that—bang on a door, with an audience, when nobody came. No, I don't think so. I'd be too embarrassed. And yet, Jesus encourages us to have this tenacious boldness in prayer. We belong on that doorstep. And we should knock and knock and knock.

But when you pray, do you ever wonder if somebody else would get a more immediate response to their knocking? I think we secretly suspect others are better at prayer than we are, better knockers. Who among us hasn't, at some point, asked somebody else to pray in the hope that God would be more inclined to listen to them: Maybe the pastor, or your saintly grandma, or that prayer warrior in church?

If praying was only for pastors or saints, Jesus would tell the masses to leave it to the experts. Instead, Jesus explains how to pray, not only to his disciples, but to a mixed crowd, people of all ages and education levels. Some in the crowd that day had likely been praying for years. Others were just learning. Jesus teaches them all, because everyone is invited to stand on God's doorstep.

Jesus says prayer is for all of us. We can all enjoy prayer, be nourished by prayer, draw close to God in prayer. All of us are welcome on God's doorstep.

Once we are on the doorstep, Jesus invites us to remember who is behind the door. He describes it in terms of relationship.

Prayer is asking your father for advice,

or going to your best friend's house for bread,

or packing lunch for your child.

When you pray, you are standing at the front door of one who loves and values you, who wants the best for you. You are not waiting for the judge, or your boss, or the king to come out. When you pray, it's like knocking at your parents' home or calling your friend in the middle of the night.

You stand on the doorstep of a familiar home.

Inside is someone who loves you.

Who will answer.

With one caveat . . . God may not respond on your timeline.

I've noticed that most of my prayers are *not* answered immediately. Jesus knows this too. And more, Jesus knows how that makes us feel, how discouraging it can be.

So Jesus says prayer is like going to a friend's house in the middle of the night. When you find yourself banging, begging, but the door is shut, and it feels like no one is even there, or if they are, they aren't coming . . . when prayer feels like that . . . keep knocking.

God will answer.

Pray for today's food, Jesus says: *what your body needs.*

Pray for forgiveness: *what your heart needs.*

Pray to resist temptation: *what your soul needs.*

And don't fold if one knock isn't enough.

In Jesus' story, the person knocking on the door at night is there for bread. He has received unexpected guests and found himself without enough food. In the ancient Near East, if you were unable to feed a guest, you failed as a host, bringing shame on yourself and your family. The person in Jesus' story is knocking on his friend's door because if he can't get the bread, he will lose social standing. Important, but not life-threatening.

Why is that person knocking late at night? To meet a social need. It's not cancer, or death, or addiction, just bread. If "just bread" is fair game for midnight, if we can bother God because we need to be hospitable, then *everything else* is fair game too. Jesus invites us to bring to God not only little social problems, but physical needs, and interior, heartfelt ones, and matters of the soul, and relationships. Every single one of our needs is worthy of God's time. Even at inconvenient hours.

I love how the NLT translates Jesus' words (Luke 11:9)—

keep on asking,

keep on seeking,

keep on knocking.

The verb tense Jesus uses is a continuous form. It indicates action that goes on over time. Think of how a three-year-old tenaciously asks for what she wants, then subtract the whining.

How do we pray? Well, Jesus says, it's like standing on a doorstep, in the middle of the night, and knocking, and knocking, and knocking, because we know the one inside loves us and *will* answer.

Come back with me to the bus stop. As God whispered to me, I saw this ancient Scripture come to life. Suddenly, I was invested. I felt like I was standing with that woman, in the dark, needing something so vital from the one inside that I refused to give up, despite the shame, despite the hour, despite the people watching.

Come on, I prayed, please open.

I need the story to end well.

For me, for you, for all of us.

There was a lot riding on that woman's faith.

And then the knocking stopped.

The door opened,

the musician stood in his bathrobe,

with something in his hand: a key.

"Glad you kept at it," he said, "I know you need this."

They hugged and she sped back to her house in her yellow golf cart.

I'm not sure why she needed that key. Or what it could have unlocked at 6:30 a.m. But she didn't give up. And he answered. And she got that key.

Prayer can be hard. I know you have given up before. Jesus knows that too. That's why he encourages his followers to stay on the doorstep—to not be ashamed, or embarrassed, or discouraged, but to *knock with hope.*

Try This

- Find a doorway where you could pray. Let it be a door to a place you love: a room in your home, the doorway to your garden, a special childhood spot, or even your church's front door. Go there and read Luke 11:5–10. What door have you been banging on for a long time? Are there prayers you have given up on? As you sit before that door, picture God on the other side. What is God doing? What does God say to you?

- When you pray, how do you picture God? An angry judge? Strict father? Someone shaking a fist at you? Experiment with seeing God differently. Pick one of these biblical metaphors—mother hen, friend, good shepherd, eagle teaching her young to fly, gifted gardener, kind daddy, nursing mother. As you pray, hold that image of God in your mind. Find a new metaphor each day this week. How does using these images of God impact your prayer?

5

God at the Galleria

Mockery and Misunderstanding

Do to others whatever you would like them to do to you.

MATTHEW 7:12

"Stop. Stop it!" The young woman coming toward me giggles in a way that negates her words. I spare the young couple a quick glance before refocusing on my phone. I'm walking fast, trying to type as I go, admittedly more focused on the screen than their conversation. At the same time, I don't want to crash into them.

Though my focus is elsewhere, part of my brain still listened. "Stop, don't be mean," she says, attempting to stifle yet another fit of giggles. He's talking loudly, like he wants to be heard. She thinks whatever he's saying is cruel, but deliciously funny. "Stop . . ." But there's a sub-text: *"Don't stop. It's cute. You're wicked. I love it."* He continues.

They're close now. So close that part of my brain registers his words, not just hers: "Gotta check social media. I'm so important. I can't live without the Kardashians. I can't even *walk* without checking Instagram." I was trying to tune him out. Trying to focus on my phone. And yet, my brain processed this stranger's words and flagged them. A bright, red flag.

Wait, my mind urged.

Stop!

You are under attack.

24

I took a few more steps. Then it hit me . . . that couple weren't just laughing in general. They were laughing at me. He was making fun of *me*. That trendy, well-dressed man had been mocking me the entire time we walked toward each other, even as we passed. Loudly, hilariously. He wanted to be heard. Wanted me to hear. Wanted all the other shoppers at that outdoor mall to overhear and laugh along, as the woman on his arm had done.

As I realized and processed what he had been doing, red-hot fury bubbled up. I was so angry that I contemplated turning on my heel and confronting him. "Hi, I'm Rev. Laura Heikes. So nice to meet you, what were you saying again?" I could show that punk what shame feels like.

Fury broke over me and I forgot all about the phone I'd been so focused on minutes before. Mercifully, he was out of reach, a retreating silhouette. Which was grace, because it gave me time to think, time to pray, time to find a better response than rage.

Anger, you see, is often the mask we often put over other, less socially acceptable emotions. When people tell me they are angry, I often gently ask what they think is behind that anger. What messier, more embarrassing emotion is the anger covering up? Because there's almost always something beneath our anger. I took a breath and asked myself: What is the emotion I actually feel? And there it was. Behind the rage lay a more vulnerable reality: I was hurt, felt embarrassed.

A stranger, with no idea who I was or why I was on my phone, laughed at me, made me the butt of his jokes. The woman with him joined in. And everyone around me overheard. My texting and walking might have been different, silly even, but I wasn't hurting anyone. I didn't crash into that man. I wasn't swerving erratically. I could have gone unnoticed. But he made me the focus of everyone's scorn. I met God at the mall on Sunday afternoon. The day two strangers laughed at me.

You won't normally find me at the mall on Sunday afternoon, because I'm just so drained from Sunday morning. A nap is almost mandatory. Especially on Sundays like the one I'd just had: preaching three worship services followed by praying with a man facing a cancer diagnosis. Then I'd hosted a group for new believers who wanted to know more about the church. I was supposed to take them to lunch, but the little group of five had chosen to just chat in the church instead. My family, who had been looking forward to a burger at the Icehouse, decided to wait. As soon as I was done, we'd go eat. I had a great session with the newbies, but as I told them goodbye, I discovered one of my church staff waiting; a church member had made inappropriate comments to her grown daughter. This was an issue that couldn't wait. We sat, talked, and decided on a plan of action.

By the time I finished, I was ready to collapse, physically and emotionally. So were my poor kids. They had waited for almost an hour and a half. They were hungry and grumpy and tired. We all were.

We went to get a burger, as promised. A little bit of good food, some time with the ones I loved, that was going to go a long way to restoring my energy and spirit. But before the food arrived, my phone buzzed. A young mother texted me—her wife was in the hospital. Emergency surgery. She was scared and alone and asked if I could come pray and sit with them. I told my kids and my husband that there was a pastoral emergency and kissed them goodbye, asking them to put my lunch in a doggy bag. Luckily, we'd taken two cars that day. I fast-walked to mine, typing a response to this scared woman as I went.

That's when two strangers saw me. And made fun of me. Loudly. Persistently. Cruelly.

I was tired and hungry and worn down, but there was an emergency, and I was headed to help. They assumed I was a clueless, self-absorbed, social media junkie.

What really took me by surprise is how much it hurt, how embarrassed I felt. I should have been able to shake it off, but I couldn't. So I talked to God about it as I continued toward my car. As I prayed, God helped me understand how often we all fall into the trap that couple did. Maybe we don't say it out loud on the sidewalks. Maybe we whisper it to a friend. Or just think it. But at some point, we have all assumed the very worst of others and treated them according to those assumptions.

I found God at the mall when two people mocked me. I met God on a sidewalk because in that moment, I realized the urgency of Jesus' call to treat others with kindness.

We live in a society that has modified the golden rule into something like: "Do to others what they have done to you." Or better yet: "Do it to them *before* they can do it to you."

It reminds me of a conversation I had with my daughter when she was going into seventh grade. When asked what excited her, she told me she was looking forward to not being the youngest one. Because, she continued with barely a breath, now she could be the one who made fun of sixth graders.

I was horrified. My sweet little girl!? What in the world?

I tried to redirect my daughter, asking, "How did that make you feel, when you were picked on?"

"Oh," she said, "I was a brat then, I probably deserved it."

"But how did it make you feel?"

"Well, terrible."

"So be *better*, choose kindness, change the story!" I almost yelled.

"You just don't understand," my tween told me with a heavy sigh and the requisite eye roll. "I was treated badly, but now I get to treat *them* badly."

Yes, all too often we default to treating other people the way we have been treated. But it's sick, a symptom of our fallen world, a trait of sin, not an attribute of God's redeemed children.

Jesus wants to heal us of this sickness. The antidote is the golden rule: treat others *the way you wish they would treat you*. Do so knowing they may never return that kindness. Do so even when they don't deserve it. Do so because that's how God always treats us. The Bible says God is kind to the wicked and ungrateful (Luke 6:35). We are his children when we teach ourselves to do the same.

Treating others as we *wish* they would treat us is an invitation to a new kind of imagination. Not what are the *worst* things I can imagine about you and your motivations, but what are the *best* reasons you might be acting this way?

My friend Danae began to live the golden rule a few years ago in the middle of a very tough marriage. Her relationship was in a terrible spot, but she didn't talk about it at work. Her coworkers did not know. Friends like me didn't know. Even her family didn't know. She saw a therapist once a week in the evenings. But beyond that, Danae carried the sorrow alone. As she shouldered that secret pain day after day, God helped her realize that others might be grappling with similar sorrows, just as hidden, and just as debilitating.

So Danae taped a reminder to her desk, "Be kind to others. You have no idea what they are going through." She wanted to see those words each day. Then, if someone was grumpy or snappish, she'd remember that she didn't know what secret pain they were shouldering. She told me that having a deep, hidden sorrow helped her realize others might too. She started to treat even the most difficult people with the kindness she wished she'd receive.

Years ago, I heard a pastor say that we are either thermometers or thermostats. Thermometers read the temperature of the room, reflecting whatever's already there. But thermostats have the power to *change* the temperature of the entire space. Jesus calls us to be thermostats. To not just reflect what's already in the world but shape it. We do that by treating others the way we long to be treated.

Try This

- Choose one person who you don't know well, but have drawn negative conclusions about, and get to know them. Find out where they grew up, what they love to do in their free time, what interesting skills or attributes they have. Ask questions, learn more, be curious. Try to leave your expectations at the door and just listen. What do you discover?

- We tend to ascribe the best motives to ourselves, but the worst to others. This week, give others the grace you give yourself. Seek to give every bad driver, every grumpy child, every lazy coworker, the benefit of the doubt. What changes in your heart as you do this?

6

Have It Your Way

God at Burger King

We want to sit in places of honor next to you,
one on your right and the other on your left.

MARK 10:37B

HAVE IT YOUR WAY? Darn right!

I love Burger King. Maybe it's their motto: the promise of something that goes completely *my* way. I don't always get my way with my husband, or my kids, or at work, or in traffic (even if I do have the right-of-way!). But when I pull up to the drive-thru window, the employees at Burger King long to make my burger exactly how I like it: cheese, lettuce, tomato, and mayo.

McDonald's doesn't get me like Burger King does. No matter how many times I try to customize their Big Mac, the burger emerges in its standard form: cheese and lettuce (okay), sauce (meh), pickles and onions (blech!).

Burger King's slogan speaks to my felt need—a burger that caters to *my* taste buds, not a standardized "normal" that theoretically suits everyone.

Burger King also appeals to my sense of adventure and creativity. They encourage you to tweak everything. Signs near the soda fountain at the Burger King by my house contain interesting suggestions on how to mix ordinary fountain drinks into exotic beverages. "Have it your way!" declares

29

the soda fountain. Some stores have alternative seating areas with couches and love seats. So you can even *sit* your way!

So mix your Dr Pepper with a splash of tea, grab a fist full of ketchup packets, and expect, nay, *demand*, that your burger emerge tuned to your specific (perfect) palate.

Burger King had always been about me and what I wanted. Until I thought to look for God there. Then, for the first time, I found myself in Burger King not to be served, but just to watch. And as I sat there waiting, looking for God, I saw things I'd never seen when I was there to be served. I saw, really noticed, the people on the other side of the counter.

Every time someone came in, a person behind the counter looked up, smiled, and asked how they could help. That employee answered questions and made suggestions. No matter who came through the door, no matter what weird thing they ordered, the worker never judged the person or their tastes. All were worthy of being treated well—everyone and anyone was served no matter how they voted, the kind of day they'd had, their last employee performance review at work, or their current relationship status.

The manager was especially kind. When I spoke to him, asking him to share crazy customer stories (you know, as color for this chapter), he told me he didn't have any bad customers. I was inclined to believe this was a blatant "party line" until he told me that when he changed stores several years ago, many of his clients switched, too, driving from nearly ten miles away. This leader's presence made getting a burger more than a business transaction.

Jesus calls a group of men who are nobodies and asks them to be leaders in the most important launch ever: God's kingdom on earth. Like most of us, the first disciples preferred standing on the ordering side of the counter. Even, it seems, after they'd been with Jesus long enough to know better. So we have this embarrassing story: Jesus is headed for Jerusalem, the capital. And on the journey, the disciples begin to jockey for the best positions in the new corporate structure, which they hope is just around the corner. "Have it your way" isn't mustard and bacon, but thrones and power! And oh, how they want it their way.

Jesus loves these men. He loves them so much he can't leave them on the wrong side of the counter. So Jesus explains God's organizational structure, "You know that the rulers in this world lord it over their people, and officials flaunt their authority over those under them. But among you it will be different. Whoever wants to be a leader among you must be your servant . . ." (Matt 20:25–26).

We are so accustomed to being on the "have it our way" side of things that faith can be jarring. Suddenly, instead of thrones, we get a dorky worker's hat. Instead of immediate answers to prayers and special privileges as God's chosen ones, Jesus says, "Give up your own way, take up your cross, and follow me" (Matt 16:24).

It goes against our nature. Heck, it goes against the nature of the whole world. The more power you have in this world, the more you get to boss everybody else around. But Jesus teaches us that with God, the more power you have, the more you will take the jobs nobody else wants. Because the better you get at serving, the better you get at faith.

On the last night of his life, Jesus' disciples are still (sigh) jostling for the best seats, the places of honor. Even Passover tables had good seats and lesser seats. The standard configuration meant about half of the disciples were going to "lose." Nobody wanted to be the low man on the totem pole. I imagine them sitting with arms crossed, casting dark looks at the people they think are lesser in status, deciding if the seating is equitable or not. Most of all, I can picture them waiting. The person with the lowest status is supposed to wash everyone's feet. Nobody thinks it should be them. I can see each one giving pointed looks to the disciple they've decided is at the bottom of the pecking order.

Just then, Jesus, who rightly sits at the head of the table, stands to take up the job everyone else thinks is below them, washing each disciple's filthy feet. Then Jesus tells them *serving* is what it means to be powerful in God's kingdom.

The first time our bishop visited my church, it was because of a disaster. A wildfire three miles from our church destroyed forty-eight homes. My congregation, miles from the epicenter, became the heart of the community response. People gathered to await news. Law enforcement met survivors in our sanctuary. The community came with supplies, food, and blankets. We stood on the hill outside the sanctuary and watched and prayed and held each other's hands as black smoke poured into the air. The fire department came and went, refilling their trucks from our water storage.

That week, the bishop drove several hours to come encourage us. By then, the burned area was starting to reopen. Families were returning to comb through debris. Very few folks were allowed in, but the pastors and bishop were permitted to go in to help, pray, and bring supplies like tools and water. I watched our bishop, whom I barely knew. He encouraged the workers, spoke with the leaders, and helped us deploy our resources.

The ground was still hot in places, and people were just getting back into their neighborhoods to see what was left of their homes. I'd introduce myself as "Pastor Laura," from the church down the road. The bishop would say, "I'm Jim." No titles. No special status. Jim was there to serve, to help, to bring hope to people who had lost everything.

One of the many people we visited was Robby. We found him by the melted wreck of his trailer home and were able to give him shovels, gloves, and cool drinking water. Robby told us how he had escaped, barely, when the fire swept in. Then he asked if we'd walk with him through his lot. He took us around the ruins of his house and finally to an area that had been his garden. Robby stopped above a little heap and broke down. As I looked closer, I could see burned feathers. "Gracie and Pepper," he sobbed, "my chickens. They loved this garden." He took a few deep breaths and managed to tell us, "I just haven't been able to bury them."

"Could we help you do it?" Jim asked. Robbie nodded. And there, in the smoking ruin, the bishop dug a grave and said a prayer for Robbie's chickens. He never said who he was or mentioned his leadership position. He just served. That was enough.

Jesus doesn't ask us to be kings and queens. He asks us to be the people a hurting world turns to when life is the very worst. He asks us to move to the other side of the counter and serve others. Wouldn't it be great if we could answer Jesus' call to serve with a smile?

Try This

- Are you used to standing on the "customer" side of counters? Take some time to sit near a place where people are served—a car wash, fast-food restaurant, ER lobby, airport terminal, or convenience store.

Notice the people on the other side, those who do the serving. Which of their attributes would Jesus commend and want to see more of in your life? In your community of faith?

- Small service, done over time, can change the world. I encourage my folks to give an hour of their time each week in service. Is there an hour you could give someplace—a food pantry, local school, thrift store, sports program, 4-H club, or nursing home? Everybody has a skill and passion that God longs to use to bless others. Perhaps you love animals, art, gardening, sports, fishing, running, or yoga. How might you serve in an area you love? Ponder how the world would change if everyone in your friendship circle, workplace, or church gave just one hour in service every week. Be the one to get it started.

7

Picking Up Chicks

God at the County Fair

One of [the Pharisees], an expert in religious law, tried to trap [Jesus] with this question: "Teacher, which is the most important commandment in the law of Moses?" Jesus replied, "'You must love the Lord your God with all your heart, all your soul, and all your mind.' This is the first and greatest commandment. A second is equally important: 'Love your neighbor as yourself.' The entire law and all the demands of the prophets are based on these two commandments."

MATTHEW 22:35–40

"I love picking up chicks!"

My three-year-old daughter Anna shouted this revelation to me (and all the nearby patrons) in the grocery store checkout line. It was one of those moments when things got very still. The man in front of us cleared his throat, nervous. No one actually turned to look, but they *wanted* to. They were all wondering—which family talked about "picking up chicks" so frequently that their toddler knew the phrase? They'd sneak a look in a minute and somebody would recognize me: "Oh my goodness! That's the *pastor's* kid!"

I let a few heartbeats of horrified silence settle as I eyed Anna, perched in the shopping cart. Where had she learned this juicy little tidbit? Wait. That didn't matter. Clarity. That's what I needed. I settled for the most basic question, "What?"

Anna, seeing that Mommy didn't share her joy, repeated her statement, "I *love* picking up chicks!" Just as loud, this time with a smile.

My eyes narrowed, pondering the likely suspects. Preschool? Neighborhood kids? Uncle Greg? Yes. It had to be my kid brother. I was going to *murder* him.

But suddenly, my husband, who had been standing mute the entire time, saved the day: "At the fair, Anna? You like picking up the *baby chicks* at the county fair?"

"Yes!" replied my little girl, "I *love* picking up those chicks." Whew.

In the purely literal sense, picking up chicks is something *everyone* in Comal County loves. Our city is home to the "Oldest County Fair in Texas." There are games, dancing, food, and competitions to see who can bake the best pie or raise the best-looking goat.

But one of the most beloved features of the Comal County Fair is that you get to belly up to an enclosure filled with hundreds of soft, yellow chicks and grab one. You are permitted, nay, *encouraged*, to hold these little drops of sunshine to your heart's content.

Weeks before that heart-stopping day in the grocery store, I held Anna's little hand as we waited in line to hold the baby chicks, inching ever closer to this town mecca. Finally, two people left and we were allowed through the gate. At the center of a fenced-off, sawdusted area was a knee-high table filled with wood shavings and at least a hundred fluffy yellow chicks.

But our delight quickly faded as Anna and I faced a harsh reality: we were terrible at picking up chicks. We were not alone in this deficiency. High-pitched peeping, kicking legs, and the determined dodging movements of terrified fluff-balls testified to the fact that most of us were picking up chicks . . . badly. Tiny legs stuck out at odd angles from over-eager hands. Feet kicked desperately. The level of disturbed peeping would occasionally crescendo if someone squeezed too hard or let go too soon.

Anna's chick immediately wiggled free of her small hands and tumbled a short distance to the shavings, lying stunned but unharmed. I held on to my own, but it was chirping frantically. I tried to pet it in what I hoped was a soothing manner while whispering what I hoped were soothing words into what I hoped were its ears.

It was at that point that a child of about seven walked over to us and said with great authority, "You are not doing it right. *This* is how you hold a chick."

I glanced at the second-grader. She wasn't part of the farm team. And she was a lot younger than people I typically look to for advice. Still, her chick was asleep in her hands. "If you hold them with *two* hands, like this," the elementary school child demonstrated, "they feel safe." She cupped both hands around the chick's body and curled her thumbs over its back. While her chick dreamed, mine peeped out a prayer to every god it knew.

I took the child's advice, adding my second hand and curving them both around the chick. The effect was instantaneous. Within a minute, my chick also slept. So yes, I, too, love picking up chicks. And I found God doing it, once I learned to use two hands.

Learning how to hold things is something we all do at some point. "Two hands!" is the go-to phrase for parents of young children. You might even hear us mumbling it in our sleep. Kevin and I are constantly saying, "Two hands!" as Asher attempts to carry his dishes to the sink. What's interesting is that when our son's second hand connects with the plate, his eyes come with it. Using two hands is not just about balance and strength, but focus.

But as we grow, we don't need to use both hands to focus on simple tasks anymore. When's the last time your spouse leaned over as the offering plate went by and said, "Two hands, dear." Quite the opposite. Most of us are proud of the number of things we can "handle" at once. For example, I can eat a taco and drive my car! I can talk on the phone and unlock my office! And I can carry more bags than a pack mule—Asher's school back-pack, my lunch, my laptop bag, my iced tea, *and* my keys. I'm often asked if I've been a waitress. Not exactly, my hands are just that *good*. I'm so grown up that I no longer need to give my whole attention to any one thing.

Overall, I'm proud of how much this allows me to get done in the least amount of time. Lots of us are proud of our ability to multitask. But I wonder if we might learn something spiritual from picking up chicks. Something about using both hands in more of our lives.

I got to hear a young woman share her experiences of visiting her parents in Hong Kong. In Asia, she discovered, it's rude to pass anything to another person with one hand. You must always pass things with two hands. This cultural value required lots of practice and mental energy. She had to remember to use both hands to give her purchase to the cashier, both hands when offering up her credit card. Suddenly small actions required all her attention. At first it was an annoyance. But she found, as she used two hands, that doing so forced her to focus on the person she was interacting with. Respect requires focus. And using two hands demands we give our whole attention to what we are doing and who we are with in that moment.

Jesus has something to say about focus. Rabbis of Jesus' day had counted 613 commands (248 positive and 365 negative) in the Bible. Most scholars in Jesus' day believed all 613 had equal weight, with no commandment more important than any other. So when the Pharisees ask Jesus, "Teacher, which is the most important commandment in the law of Moses?" (Matt 22:36), it's a trick question. They'll use it to confront Jesus with one of the 612 commandments he's inadvertently deemed "less important."

Unlike Pharisees, Jesus has no problem sorting out what matters most. Of all those 613, Jesus focuses on two: love God with your whole being and love your neighbor as yourself (paraphrase of Matt 22:37–40). In county fair terms, these are the "two hands" we use when living out our faith.

Jesus knows us. He knows we are used to giving partial attention to a lot of stuff. He asks us, then, to love God and others with all we have. To stop living scattered lives with 613 things that carry equal importance and focus instead on the two things that matter most.

But how do I do that when I have a mortgage, and a broken dishwasher, and a job, and rebellious kids, and a fraying marriage? We can begin by giving God our full attention at the start of each day. Just like learning to pick up a chick, it will take time and practice. Try this—set aside space in your day, early or late if it's noisy and distracting around your home, to read the Bible, pray, and talk to God. I tell my folks to try for an hour a week, or about ten minutes a day. You can build from there (and you'll want to!). Think of this time as something you won't multitask. Know that you are giving your hands, both of them, to God. Give God every bit of you and let God hold all of you right back in those minutes. Don't get discouraged or frustrated. If you are distracted, just refocus, take a breath, and start afresh.

Once we learn how to be fully present with God, to give God our heart, soul, mind, and strength, the next part will flow from it—giving others the same focused love.

Start with your family. Do you come home and plop in front of the TV? Do you zone out with your phone? A little of that is okay, sure, but your family needs both your hands, your full attention. Give it to them. Your full attention, love, and focus are one of the greatest gifts you can give. Put down the phone, turn off the TV, and listen to your child, play a game together, go out for coffee with your spouse, make a meal together. Hold the people you love with two hands, and you'll be amazed at how much peace fills your home.

From there you might ask—how do I treat other people? A while back, my home experienced foundation problems. In the course of the repair, which we had to pay for out-of-pocket, much of our plumbing cracked. Insurance would help with that, but we were so financially drained that I needed to get my claim check before I could afford to pay the plumber to come. I'd been waiting a week (which is a long time without a toilet or shower, friends) when I finally heard back from the insurance agent. She had been out of the office, she explained. I imagined her vacationing while my family and I showered at the YMCA. But then she added: "I was taking care of my mother," before quickly pivoting back to the claim. We were on the way to what I needed—that check. But something inside perked up to remind me that a sick mother was a greater trial than my plumbing woes. So I pushed aside my need and asked—"How is your mother?" She didn't say much, but that was the right thing to do. I will do that again. I will remember not only what I need, but what others need, and hold them as carefully as I want to be held.

This won't be easy, my taco-eating-driving-texting friends. But if we can manage to put away the cell phone, to turn off the TV, to ignore social media, and to give both hands to God and those around us, it will be beautiful. We'll be glad we did.

I know because when I succeed, it's memorable. I remember the night Anna and I were stuck waiting at the Quarry in San Antonio. We'd been there a few hours, shopping. Soon my brother would arrive to take us to my mom's house for dinner.

The Quarry is a cool place—a shopping center in what used to be an old limestone mining pit. I can still remember driving by the abandoned mine as a kid and staring at the impossibly deep crater in the earth, littered with rusting equipment and edged with spooky abandoned buildings. These days, those buildings house chic stores and the crater is a fancy golf course.

Anna and I were all shopped out, so we sat on a stone bench to wait. I remembered my goal of holding whatever time I had with two hands, so I put my phone away and sought to just be present, on the bench, with my daughter. After only a minute, Anna pointed—birds! I followed her little finger to see starlings lined up along rooftops. As I took time to look, I realized the birds were covering trees and wheeling through the air in great undulating clouds. The sound of all those wings, the soft song of their voices, was magical. I wondered—had this beauty been here in the Quarry the whole time? The entire afternoon, my entire life? And I only just noticed it? How does that happen?

Too often we miss the beauty around us. We miss it because we're so fragmented and scattered. Jesus gives us a better way: the two commandments that matter most. It all boils down to this: how you hold the chicks at the county fair is how you should hold onto God and those around you: with two hands.

Try This

- Practice handing things to others using two hands. Try doing this for an entire day—never pass something to anyone using only one hand. What are your observations about this experience?

- Choose a day this week when you'll be fully present wherever you are. Keep your phone dark, don't try to distract yourself with music or a podcast, just be in that moment, with that person, or even alone. What do you notice that you might have missed otherwise?

- Set your alarm ten minutes earlier this week. When you wake up, don't pick up your phone. Take a few deep breaths, smile, and spend the first part of your day talking to God. Read a Bible passage, pray, listen. Give God your full attention with joy. Notice any difference in your days when you begin this way.

8

Stuck in Line

Discovering God in Small Trials

Keep watch and pray, so that you will not give in to temptation.
For the spirit is willing, but the body is weak!

MATTHEW 26:41

ONE, TWO, THREE, SIX, TEN, TWELVE people in line ahead of me . . . how can there possibly be this many people *grocery shopping* on Friday night? We'd swung by the Safeway near my mom's house in Colorado to grab a few necessities for the next morning. It was 9 p.m. in the tiny town of Estes Park, population 6,377. But the lines looked like a blizzard was about to hit.

My husband and I had *two* items: nondairy milk and a container of soy yogurt. Both were absolutely necessary for my toddler's breakfast the next morning. Before you ask, we were already *in* the "fifteen items or fewer" line! And all the other lines were worse. True, it wasn't like I had somewhere else to be (except *bed*). I just deeply resented waiting in line for an eternity when the errand should have taken five minutes, tops.

My brain was not helping; the thoughts there only made it worse! How did this store not plan for a rush? Surely *they* know the times they'll be busy? This crush of people at 9 p.m. caught me off guard, but *they* must know . . . could they not staff up!? Now I'm stuck here, held hostage by the bozo at the front of the express line who swears the ice chest he's buying was labeled $19.99 even though it's ringing up $89.99. He won't rest until one

40

of the much-needed workers finds a second blasted ice chest to do a price check. This man is not backing down—he is now demanding photographic proof of the signage around the chest.

I wish I were kidding.

Kevin and I waited. And waited. Each of the other lines was equally clogged. Ugh! I was so angry, which is when I realized something needed to change, but it wouldn't be on the store's end. It had to be *me*. I needed an immediate change of heart. To do this, I decided to fall back on something I love. I would look for God in the grocery store. This could keep me from turning into a full-on rage monster.

But here's the rub—I couldn't see God! Even though I was looking and praying, nothing. I considered each person in front of me, behind me. I considered the long lines around me, the bright lights, the store itself. Nothing. I looked at the products around me, the items in people's carts. Still nothing. I sighed, realizing that God wasn't missing, but something within me was thwarting my ability to see God.

I attempted to refocus my heart and kept at it. When we finally reached the front of the line, I engaged the checker in conversation, and he informed me that we were standing in the "busiest grocery store in the nation." I assume he meant the busiest *Safeway* in the nation, but perhaps that little grocery store at the foot of the Rocky Mountains really is the all-time national grand champion of congestion. Whatever. I believed him. The checker told me it would stay frantic until the store closed at 12 a.m., at which time they would have to lock the doors to keep people out. The unkind part of my mind began to think—"And you didn't *staff up*!?" I shushed it. I wanted to meet God at the worst grocery store in the nation and being angry wasn't helping.

I got my change, but strangely, I wasn't ready to leave. I still hadn't seen God. Something within me was still blinding me. God was there, there was a sign, some evidence, some note of love from God to the people in this store. After all, there is no place on earth without a witness to God (Acts 14:17). I couldn't leave. So I sweet-talked my long-suffering husband, Kevin, into sitting down to watch and look. We perched on the high barstools at a Starbucks kiosk in the front of the store. As we simply watched, I noticed something. I was not the only person suffering. There were other people demanding price checks while those in line behind them ground their teeth. One woman swore loudly at the workers, and then laughed to her friend that she delighted in being a problem. Ugh. There were definitely worse lines than the ice-chest price check. None moved quickly. And the people? Some people showed patience, others played on their phones. Some were clearly losing their minds.

And then I met God at the busiest grocery store in the nation, as I heard God's call to practice my faith in spaces I don't like.

The last night of his life, Jesus takes his disciples with him to the Garden of Gethsemane. He asks them to be with him. To pray for him. Watch and pray, he says. Watch and pray (Matt 26:41).

The disciples fail at both.

They stop watching.

They stop praying.

They fall asleep.

It was a terrible, difficult, challenging space—that dark olive grove. Jesus, their leader, is in agony; they can see it, can hear him crying. But they are utterly unable to help. Unable to even do what he asks. They can't watch. They don't pray. They just . . . go to sleep.

Now wait a minute. What in the world does this huge moment in salvation history have to do with the mild annoyance of standing in line?

Lines, and other frustrating places, are chances to *practice* our faith. They are not big moments like Gethsemane, but small-scale trials. Trials that give us an opportunity to deal with situations beyond our control. We are made to wait, we encounter frustrations and setbacks, we are often powerless to change the situation or help ourselves. Yes—you and I can use lines to practice our faith!

How? Do what Jesus asks: watch and pray.

First, the watching. The disciples kept falling asleep. Do you ever "fall asleep" in challenging situations? I have a friend who jokes that if he's not careful, he really will go to sleep to escape the pressure of looming deadlines. Others of us "go to sleep" by pulling out our phones, popping in ear buds, or turning on our favorite show. We zone out to deal with discomfort. How often is the TV going in the background of your life? Or the news? How long do you ever wait nowadays before you pull out your phone? I have seen multiple people in my town, not just texting at stoplights, but watching videos and shows on their phones! The next time you're in line, notice how many people mitigate that small discomfort with technology.

To meet God, put away your phone, avoid the magazines, and notice what's around you. Keep watch, Jesus says. You can practice in lines. You'll be there only a handful of minutes. Ask God to meet you, to speak to you or through you. See where you are. Think of your community, think of the people, think of their needs. Think of how God loves each person waiting with you.

I gave it a try, putting my phone away and opening my heart to God in line. As I did, some interesting things happened. In line at my local grocery store, I admitted to the checker that I was buying a small variety of toddler squeeze packs because I'd forgotten to pack my son's dinner. I said something offhand about failing as a mother. "Oh, seriously," he told me, "don't worry. I hear parents say that all the time. You've solved it! Congratulate yourself!" I smiled back at this high school student. What a gift!

Another day, I let a frazzled woman go in front of me. And on another, I chatted with a man buying cigarettes. Angels didn't burst from the metal rafters trailing excited sparrows, but guess what? I actually *remember* standing in those lines, meeting those people. It's a fun challenge—to stay awake, to look for God.

When you are in line, stuck in traffic, waiting at the doctor's office, or the DMV, or the airport, whatever small inconvenience life throws at you, watch. Just watching and being aware will transform that experience.

The other thing Jesus asks his disciples to do is pray. The first of Jesus' instructions, to stay awake and watch, helps you engage with *others* and the space around you. This second suggestion, to pray, invites *God* into that place!

Are you waiting forever for your food to come out? Did some bozo just cut in front of you at airport security? Is everyone around you über-grumpy and unloading on the increasingly frazzled barista? Invite God into that tricky space. Pray for the person in front of you. Pray for the checker or waiter or service personnel. Pray for a stressed parent. Or a drained person in scrubs. Look around. Is someone adding up what they have in the cart, subtly calculating if they have enough money? Pray for them, please. Invite God into the lives of the strangers around you.

When you start to pray while stuck in line, you will begin to see those around you as people, not obstacles. If you pray every time you find yourself in line, imagine the blessings you'll be inviting into those spaces! We'll be praying in places most of us never think to pray about, or for. To me, this is the most exciting aspect.

Imagine if every believer resolved to pray each time we were in line at the grocery store! Can you even picture the power that would pour into our communities if Christians didn't pull out their phones or grab a magazine, but prayed for the people around them, the place they were stuck, the ones who worked there?

Imagine how redeeming gridlock might become! In my town, one of our main roads passes right by the local high school. It can take thirty minutes to go three miles if school is about to start or has just let out. I've told my congregation that when they get stuck in that traffic, they should pray for the students and teachers at the school. They may know some by name; they may not. But if eight hundred people start praying when they are stuck in lines or traffic, God will break through in new ways.

If all of us started to pray in line, in traffic, at the DMV, and airport security, can you even imagine what God would do? The amazing things that would happen?

First, we'd all likely double our prayer time! Hundreds more prayers would be lifted every day. Plus, all our "stuck in line" prayers would have a tremendous, maybe even miraculous impact. If every believer in your community prayed in line, how many voices would be lifting your city to God each day? All we have to do is use time we already have to connect with our loving Creator.

Lines don't have to be lost, ruined time. Do as Jesus instructs his disciples: watch and pray. When you do this, you'll turn a minor inconvenience into a way for God to transform you, your community, and the world.

Try This

- This week, turn waiting into a spiritual exercise. Pray any time you are stuck somewhere: traffic, the grocery store, the pharmacy, school pick-up line. For one week, put away your phone and watch and pray instead. Notice the people around you, waiting and working. Consider the community you are in—who calls this their home? Who drives or rides the bus or subway to work here? What kids go to school here? Pray for the people, the workers, the community. Keep a rough estimate of how much additional prayer time you have this week.

- We often ask Jesus to go with us on big, important days: when we ask for a raise, take a child to college, go in for tests. But what about the small ones? Most of our days are made up of ordinary, repetitive moments: work, meals, chores, maybe a hobby or workout. Jesus offers to go with us throughout all our days. Today, look for and expect Jesus' presence in your most ordinary moments, and ask yourself where God is just then.

9

I Pledge Allegiance

Finding God at School

But you are not like that, for you are a chosen people. You are royal priests, a holy nation, God's very own possession. As a result, you can show others the goodness of God,
for he called you out of the darkness into his wonderful light.
"Once you had no identity as a people;
now you are God's people.
Once you received no mercy;
now you have received God's mercy."

1 PETER 2:9–10

"I PWEDGE AWEGIANCE, to the fwag, of the United States of America . . ." Little voices join as, hands over heart, students recite the pledge of allegiance at the start of a crisp Monday morning one fall. I was visiting a kindergarten class, looking for God.

The students at my church suggested I look for God at school. While the suggestion wasn't as edgy as most of the suggestions I get, I had to admit how challenging a place school can be. Whether you had a positive or negative experience, most of us wouldn't want to return to live it out again. I took up the challenge, visiting schools of all levels: a college, a high school, an elementary school, and middle school (even hardened adventurers like me quail before middle school). What surprised me was that the students at every campus seemed to be trying to answer the *exact* same question: "Who am I?"

And their peers were more than happy to chip in their two cents. The one thing all those schools shared was the rampant labeling I observed. Some are obvious and acceptable: every grade has a number or a name from kinder to senior. Other labels are more subjective, based on aspects beyond that student's control: intelligence, weight, skin color, clothes, the car that picks you up, the fact that you must ride the bus. At one school, all lunches were subsidized, but students who ate the school food were ridiculed as "poor."

By high school, the labels had become so obvious that I could have almost named the "type" I saw at each table, grouped with others in their "set": athletes, rednecks, nerds, band kids, populars, thugs, stoners, drama kids, anime-lovers, computer geeks, gamers. And in each community, you might find new labels. San Angelo had "kickers" but in McAllen it's *tlacuache*, a word for "possum."

So many labels . . . affixed to each student like Post-it notes that everyone in every hallway is always reading and updating.

You and I, we have them too. We never age out of this little human quirk. Right now, you've got invisible labels all over you. They describe your behavior, the crowd you hang out with, your job, your marital status, your social standing. Some of those Post-its we've tried to stick on ourselves. Some we like and have cultivated over the years. Some we loathe.

But how close do any of those labels get to our true names? Our true selves? Is what people say *about* us really who we *are*? As I looked for God in school, I realized that many adults are still working away, trying to answer that question from our own school days: "Who am I?" Underneath the labels attached to us by friends, rivals, teachers, bosses, even parents and family members, is there an identity that is deeper? A God-sized name?

On the Monday morning I visited kindergarten, the kids learned about long and short *o* sounds. Afterwards, they each drew an octopus. I walked from table to table, admiring colorful pictures of sea creatures. Every child had their own style, but each wanted to know what *I* thought of their art. Was it good? Did I like it? "Teacher" (all female adults are "teachers" in kinder), "come see mine! Teacher, look!"

At recess, all the kids wanted me to watch them do different activities: slip down the big purple slide, climb up a jungle gym, or sprint from one end of the school yard to the other. I did, mindful to find something to praise for each child.

Carlos asked me to watch him on the monkey bars, which were formed in a very long curve, like an *8* with an extended middle. Carlos stretched his thin arms bar by bar, dodging children parked on different areas of the structure, sometimes taking several bars at a time to make it. When he was done, he hung, swinging proudly back and forth on the last bar, right in front of me. "Wow!" I said. Carlos was strong for his slight frame.

"You know," he said, talking to me as he continued to swing back and forth, "at my old elementary school, they called me 'Loser.'"

"No," I said, my heart breaking for this child.

"Yep," he insisted, meeting my eyes, "they called me 'Loser' and 'Zero.'"

"Do they call you that here?" I asked, concerned.

"No, *here* they call me 'Tough Guy.'" He seemed proud.

I could see why. Carlos clearly hated the old labels and was working hard to shake them. But while "Loser" didn't capture the spunky kid before me, neither did "Tough Guy." Without thinking, I blurted out: "What would you call yourself? Who are you in your heart?"

I immediately realized my error. I had asked Carlos a question most adults are still working on. It was way too hard for a six-year-old. But just as I was about to switch topics, he said something I'll never forget. Something way too wise for his handful of years: "I am God's child. That's who I am."

This amazing six-year-old knew something about himself that many grown-ups are still working on. He knew his identity beyond the labels others gave to him.

I discovered God at school in Carlos, who knew his deepest self: "I am God's child." In that moment at recess, I found where God was at school. God brushes off all the paper labels and gives us a name nobody can take away: "My child."

Think about these questions: What labels are sticking to you, right now? Who put them there? Which do you like? Which hurt? Now think about this: Who are you really? Deep down inside . . . the "you" that others may not take time to see?

God offers you an identity that will shape your life. To claim this core identity will sweep away all the words others have said, like a bunch of flimsy Post-it notes. To claim your God-given identity is to have a name that can never be tarnished or taken, a name you never grow out of.

God is at school, at work, at home when you answer the question of identity by saying, "I am God's child!" Allow that to be the identity that shapes your life. Then you'll know all the rest of the labels are just so many stickers. When you root yourself in being God's child, you will be that person, wherever you are. And you will shape your world, instead of it shaping you.

Speaking of being God's children wherever we are, take a deep breath my friends. It's time to look for God in Judea, those places that stretch and challenge us to move a bit beyond our typical comfort zone.

Try This

- Grab a stack of Post-it notes and write down all the names, titles, slurs, labels, and words people have stuck to you over the years. Add in the names you've attempted to cultivate for yourself. One by one, affix them to your clothes. Spend some quiet time just looking at all those names. Then ask God to set you free from all labels others have affixed to you.

- Peel the Post-its off and crumple them into the trash. Spend a little more time in quiet contemplation. God writes a new name for us (Rev 2:17), putting it into our hands on a white stone, the symbol of victory and being set free. What name is God putting into your hands? Child, Beloved, Friend, Forgiven, Fearless, something else?

Judea
Called beyond the Comfortable

10

Shampoo, Half-Full

Meeting God in an RV Bathroom

And the Lord came and called as before, "Samuel! Samuel!"
And Samuel replied, "Speak, your servant is listening."

1 SAMUEL 3:10

PERHAPS I SHOULDN'T HAVE been surprised to meet God in the bathroom. When I was growing up, the bathroom was the only room in our home with a locking door. Once I punched that scuffed gold button, I lingered, even if my little sister was waiting (sorry, Amy). Maybe that's why two of my most powerful experiences with God as a young person happened in that little room. Once, while I was brushing my teeth. Once, when I was washing my face. The bathroom was the only truly private space I had. I talked to God there a lot.

But it's been a long time since I met God in the bathroom. I have my own home now and I can find quiet, private spaces without resorting to the commode. I was not looking for God that night in the RV park, just a way to rinse the dirt off.

I was at the tail end of a family RV trip through Yellowstone. Four adults and two kids stuffed into a rented motor home. We'd been traveling through the park for nine days. We were *baked*.

The campgrounds where we parked the RV had become progressively worse. Our first site had included mini-golf and country club showers. Near the middle of the trip, we stayed in more rustic sites nestled among tall pine trees. This last stop was the low point: a huddle of tents and RV slots on the road that led to the Billings airport.

The "bathroom" by our campsite was a porta potty that even my sturdy husband deemed unsuitable. "Do *not* go in there," he soberly advised the girls and me. Kevin is fairly liberal-minded when it comes to bathrooms, so we heeded his warning and trekked the half mile up to the permanent restroom: wooden doors with hook-and-eye latches, showers with hair in the drain, and a general "community pool locker room" feel.

I showered our over-tired girls, walked them back to the RV, put them to bed, and wearily made the trek back up the hill. Some nice hot water would be perfect. Then I'd turn the kitchen table into my bed and go to sleep. But as I finished washing my hair, I felt a nudge. Just a little inner suggestion, the whisper of the Spirit: I should give my shampoo away.

Over the years, I've learned when such nudges are God, and when it's just beans. This was God, but I was completely stumped as to why God would care about my half-used shampoo. Or *who* God might want me to give it to. It was a rather insulting thing to offer someone: a half-full bottle of Suave.

I sat the shampoo beside the sink as I brushed my teeth and eyed it. Why God would be asking me to give this away? And to whom? Maybe that family in the camper next door? They had a lot of kids, maybe they'd be practical enough to not feel patronized? The landlord? They had taken our bear spray to pass on, but what would they say to a half-empty bottle of cheap shampoo? Maybe I could just leave it on the counter?

Who in the world did God want me to give this to?

Just then, a lady came in with her son. He wore footie pajamas. They were brushing their teeth too.

Maybe they wanted my shampoo? It seemed like a good choice. If they were insulted, I could leave quickly. So I introduced myself, and the mother said her name was Elaine. I screwed up my courage and asked Elaine if she wanted my shampoo. She stopped what she was doing and looked at me. Then, with total sincerity, asked if I was sure I wanted to part with it.

Jesus says we will meet him in disguise (Matt 25:31ff). I have. The woman in the smelly bathroom told me that she and her family lived at a campsite down the way. Not in an RV, but a tent. Her husband, a licensed plumber, had lost his job and was having trouble finding work. The bank had taken their home after they failed to make the payments. Elaine held back tears as she told me that just two days before, she and her husband had put their older son on a plane to go stay with his grandparents. "I don't know what we'll do," she said sadly. "I never thought we'd be living in a tent."

I gave her the shampoo and said good night and walked with a heavy heart back to my campsite. It was only August. And yet that night, the temperature would dip down into the low thirties. I opened the door to our warm, cozy RV. We had a bathroom, electricity, a fridge. They had a few nylon walls, a sleeping bag, and those footie pajamas.

It was late and we'd be leaving at 6 a.m., but when I shared the story, the four adults began to plan. We emptied the cooler of our drinks and filled it back up: soap, peanut butter, chocolate bars, cereal, granola—all our remaining food. The kids woke up and added Capri Suns and the last of their treats. Then we added a cook pot, a wool blanket, and the little Hibachi grill we'd bought for our journey. We filled an envelope with every bit of cash we had left and stuck it in with the candy bars.

Since it was so late, my brother-in-law and I walked the cooler back up the hill to the office and left it with the park owners for Elaine. They told us what a nice family this was and how hard they worked.

God found me in an RV bathroom. God spoke to me about a bottle of shampoo. Because God needed me to help Elaine and her family in their time of need.

Don't think that it'll always be *you* finding God. If you have an open heart, *God* will find you . . . in places you never expect. God will find you because God needs to help someone, and knows you'll listen. God will find you because God needs to give hope to someone who's about to give up.

Walk through your life with your eyes and ears open. God will find you wearing faces you'd never recognize. God will find you, nudge you, invite you to share something, to say something, to do something. When God whispers and you respond, a half-empty bottle of shampoo can become a moment of grace.

Try This

- The next time a person randomly pops into your head, give them a call or text them. You might say, "You were on my mind. How are you?" or "I was thinking of you. How could I pray for you?" Notice what happens. You'll be surprised how often that person admits that they are going through a hard time or needed some encouragement just then. Make note of the times someone needed you. Whatever that nudge felt like—that's the voice of God! As you continue, you'll learn how God's voice sounds and more readily respond with "yes," even when it feels uncomfortable.

- Samuel didn't know how to hear God's voice until Eli taught him (1 Sam 3). Samuel's prayer, "Speak, Lord, for your servant is listening," is a great way to invite God to speak to you. Pray this prayer every day this week, then keep your spiritual ears open.

11

Edges

The Divine in Modern Art

When you gather the grapes in your vineyard, don't glean the vines after they are picked. Leave the remaining grapes for the foreigners, orphans, and widows. Remember that you were slaves in the land of Egypt. That is why I am giving you this command.

DEUTERONOMY 24:21-22

I'M STARING AT TWO completely blank canvases on the wall of the Blanton Museum of Art in Austin.

Blank.

Totally white.

Nothing.

What in the world? I bend to read the card next to this "art" and see "Most sensation is on the edges of things." My gaze shifts and I realize these pictures are *not* blank. The art just isn't where I expected it to be.

As I perused the artwork in Austin's Blanton Museum, I noticed an interesting transition. In centuries past, most art was religious. Mary and Jesus, Jesus and the disciples, the crucifixion, the apostles. The Blanton has rooms of art where God's work and love are the subject. As the centuries pass,

57

though, God is less and less frequently the subject of the artist's focus. Until that blank canvas . . .

It was in the modern art section, which contains some remarkable pieces: a looped video of a woman singing "Under Pressure" to herself in a tiny airplane bathroom in a costume made of toilet paper, seat liners, towels, and other airplane paraphernalia. I was impressed, but deeply grateful I wasn't the person waiting in line behind her on that transatlantic flight. I saw a tribute to a civil rights leader made from plastic combs. A sea of copper pennies below a sky of bones. And lots of color.

Then I came to the empty canvases. And I paused. My cynical brother piped up, "This artist is clearly a master. She has convinced the Blanton to buy two *blank* canvases. Behold," he gestures dramatically to the canvases, "a modern artist at the top of her game!"

I didn't have a ready retort to my brother's typical objection to modern art ("I could do/paint/create this myself"). Hmmm. This piece stumped me. How were two *blank* canvases art? I bent to read the explanation and was delightfully surprised. The card instructed me to look, not at the center of the canvas, but at the edges. This was where the artist, Jo Baer, had worked, because to her, "Most sensation is on the edge of things."

Baer realized a truth about human beings: we focus on the center without thinking. In fact, we almost *exclusively* focus on the center. Baer therefore decided to favor the edges, demanding we notice a place we typically ignore. As I looked closer, I realized that what I had assumed was the frame, was art! On the edges of her canvas, Baer painted a thick black border. Within that, a narrow line of shining gold. Gold at the edges. To draw our attention away from the favored center.

Wow!

Sensation at the edges. An artist who leaves the center blank to make us look outward, knowing we never will otherwise. That's where I found God. Because God is another artist who loves the edges!

Throughout the story of salvation, God focuses on the edges and the people there. God doesn't choose the mighty Egyptians to form a new nation, but their slaves. God doesn't pick one of David's strong older brothers to be king, but the runt. God doesn't send Jesus to a couple in the palace, but to a couple in a stable. When Jesus picks his twelve apostles, he doesn't call the names of the powerful, educated, or elite. He calls fishermen, tax collectors, and even a former zealot! "Nobodies" are the foundation of God's saving work.

God loves the edges and the people there: widows, orphans, foreigners, the poor, the lost, the sick, the broken. And God wants to help us not just *see* the people on the edges, but to love them, engage with them.

At the doorway to the promised land, God shares community expectations with the people; how they are to live as they take possession of the land. These are the values God wants the faithful to hold dear. Chief among them is the care they are to show the vulnerable: widows, orphans, aliens, and the poor.

The groups God names are outside the usual safety nets of society. Widows in that day had no voice, no honorable way to earn money, no way to seek justice if someone abused or took advantage of them. Orphans had even less, if that's possible, they had lost their parents, their providers, the ones who would take care of them. They were children without a protector, relying on distant family to take them in, to treat them well. Foreigners had been displaced from their homes by crisis or personal loss. They resided in Israel but weren't citizens. The poor were simply those who, in an age of scarcity, were at the utter bottom.

God's chosen people are to see the people on the edges and respond in love. The actions God requests are both practical and financial. The people will rest one day of the week and make sure that everyone in their household, including servants, is given the same gift. They will allow widows and aliens into their fields and vineyards and orchards to glean, which means to pick up fallen grain and fruit. God's people are also to leave the edges of their fields and vineyards unharvested so that foreigners, widows, and orphans can gather the grapes, olives, grain, and fruit growing there.

I worry about our society sometimes. I worry about our churches. I worry that we quickly remember that God loves us, but forget God's call to care for those on the edges:

Illegal immigrants,
The poor,
Orphans,
Single parents,
Grandparents raising kids,
Senior citizens trying to live on Social Security checks,

Veterans suffering alone with PTSD,
Those who fear being pulled over by the police,
Or holding the hand of their spouse at a funeral,
Or kneeling when the national anthem plays.

Society teaches us to look to the center, to long to be there, to push and pull and claw our way as close to it as we can.

But God asks us to swim against that strong current. To face outward. And not just see the edges, but make our home there.

Most sensation is at the edges of things.

God's eyes are often on the people there.

God wants ours there too.

Try This

- Who are the people on the edges of your community? Our eyes often slide past these spaces, so you may have to work to see them. Once you do, choose one person to get to know a little better.

- While most of us don't feel like we're at the center of the circle, we all have some power to see and include someone a little farther outside. What can you do to make your family, your neighborhood, or your church a more welcoming place for someone else? What power do you have that might be used to help someone on the outside?

12

People of Walmart

God in the Modern Marketplace

There is no longer Jew or Gentile, slave or free, male and female. For you are all one in Christ Jesus.

GALATIANS 3:28

I swore off Walmart the day a monster truck flattened my groceries.

For years, Walmart and I had been in a toxic relationship. But though the breakup had been building for a while, I just kept going back.

Less than a mile from my house!

Everything you need under one roof!

Prices even a pastor can afford!

And yet . . . the criminal lack of customer service, the chaotic layout, the sticky floors, the ubiquitous screaming kids (okay, those are mine). My life would be better without Walmart. But I couldn't stay away. The love-hate relationship finally tipped the day a monster truck squished my conditioner.

I was at the end of a two-hour shopping slog. I pushed the cart with the creaky wheel out the doors and blinked, troll-like, at the bright sun. My girls were whining, but we had almost crossed the finish line. There was our car. I'd unload the bags, buckle each little one into her car seat, and escape.

I had just a few bags left to put in the trunk when the plastic of a particularly heavy-laden bag tore. Groceries tumbled to the ground like victims of a blast. Damn it! Peaches and canned soup lay scattered on the hot asphalt (only *Walmart* would sack ripe peaches with canned soup). The cans survived. The peaches looked terminal.

I tried to keep one hand on the cart that held my girls as I gathered my food from the grimy parking lot. My one splurge, a bottle of fancy conditioner, which had also (apparently) been deemed "peach-friendly," rolled lazily out of my reach into the center of the parking lane. From the other end of that roadway, I heard an ominous sound: the engine of a giant monster truck, roaring toward us. I waved my arms frantically at the driver, pointing to my fancy conditioner, marooned in its path. "Noooooo!" screamed my four-year-old, who understood.

The truck didn't even slow down. Its massive tire connected with the plastic bottle and squashed it flat. As it died, my conditioner made a loud, wet sound, spraying white liquid across the hot asphalt.

I should have laughed. I should have cut my losses and escaped, but instead, I snatched up bits of broken bottle, stuffed them into the torn sack, slammed the trunk closed and prayed the milk and eggs could wait a little longer. Then I pushed the wobbly cart with my very cranky children back inside to the deepest pit of Walmart hell: customer service. After fifteen minutes, my turn came. Instead of sympathy or apology, the clerk laughed. My mouth became a hard, flat line. She looked concerned. I felt a glimmer of hope—she must feel bad for being mean. But no . . .

"This bottle doesn't have a return sticker."

You know, the sticker they give you at the front door when you return an item? I hadn't thought that really applied in this situation. But the Walmart clerk insisted that it *did*. She made me push my squeaky cart with my cranky kids back to the front to the greeter, who didn't quite know where to put the little pink sticker on the mangled, sloppy mess, but gamely applied it anyway. Then I had to wait in line. *Again*.

Which I did.

And then vowed to never return.

Ever.

Walmart and I were *done*.

Until God called me back. Not to shop—to look for signs of the divine in a maze of the commercial (a place that is about as far from the holy as I can imagine).

I often bring my church along with me as we discover God in everyday locations. Lots of people volunteer when I'm looking for God at the river or the county fair. Even the local bar draws a crowd. But *nobody* signed up for Walmart. I went alone. I sat on one of those plastic-coated metal benches and watched. Computers beeped as items were scanned. The dull murmur of conversation filled the large, open space. A few ubiquitous sparrows zoomed around the rafters.

After about five minutes, I started to notice something I had never seen on my shopping trips: the people around me. Such a spectrum of folks all jumbled up in line together. People who would never encounter each other at work, home, or school queued up without regard to any of the barriers that normally separate them.

When I mentioned I'd be searching for God at Walmart, my inbox filled up with links to websites like www.peopleofwalmart.com. One family sent me a Walmart bingo card I could print and use to pass the time. Find five squares in a row and you're a winner: a six-year-old in footie pajamas, a man under thirty with no teeth, a pregnant lady with a tramp stamp, someone trying to be Rainbow Brite, and a Nascar family. Bingo!

I cringed when I opened those emails and saw people turned into jokes and bingo squares. But, as it turns out, that's exactly where God met me at Walmart. As I looked at the diversity in the checkout line, the Holy Spirit spoke to me, reminding me of the bingo card email. Imagine, God whispered, that you took a Walmart bingo card to your church. Same people. Same goal. Could you win? Could you even get one square?

Paul tells Christians, "There is no longer Jew or Gentile, slave or free, male and female. For you are all one in Christ Jesus" (Gal 3:28). In the early church, faith tore down walls that divided people by social standing, gender, and economic situation. Very different people became united by a common love of Jesus Christ.

I'm proud of the growing diversity at my church. But the checkout line at Walmart shamed me. Little of the diversity I see in Walmart is visible in my church family. That makes me wonder: Is this diversity missing at church because these folks are not interested in God, or because God's people see them as the punch line of a joke?

We need to think carefully about our hearts, about how often we ridicule others so we can feel better, about whether making fun of people who don't wear the latest fashions or have all their teeth might trickle down into an attitude of disdain for those who are unlike us, and whether any of this lines up with following a humble Savior.

In Phil 2:3 we hear the challenge, "Don't be selfish; don't try to impress others. Be humble, thinking of others as better than yourselves." That's the way Jesus rolls. He is God, but he puts on skin, lives in this fallen world, and dies the death of a criminal, all to save our wretched souls. Seriously, who are we to put on airs with each other?

And who's to say any of us is above a bingo slot?

When I was pregnant with our third child, my swollen feet got so bad I had to purchase knee-high compression socks. I had the cringy (but utterly necessary!) habit of wearing compression socks with shorts and Adidas shower shoes—the only footwear that still fit. My older children groaned. And I knew why—I looked terrible. But it was 104 degrees outside that summer. When you're nine months pregnant in the Texas heat, fashion sacrifices must be made.

One day, as my husband and I ran the very last errands before the baby came, I commented that we wouldn't have to go to Walmart after all and breathed a sigh of relief. "Oh, honey," my husband said as he wrapped his arm around me, "I'm so glad we're not going to Walmart. Somebody might have taken your picture and posted it on peopleofwalmart.com." I looked down and was forced to agree. I was easy fodder for a bingo square that day.

Tell me you've never left the house looking like the swamp thing, wearing socks (or shoes!) that don't match, or with some green stuff stuck in your teeth. Tell me you've never had to run into the store even though you were in your swimsuit. Or picked up a prescription when you were so sick you had barely bathed. Tell me you've never accidentally walked around with your fly down or your skirt tucked into your underwear. Every one of us is fodder for ridicule on the wrong day. And on those bad, dark days, wouldn't we rather be treated with love?

We will never see a woman dressed as Rainbow Brite or a child without shoes or a pregnant lady with compression socks in our churches unless we recognize our own prejudice and, in the name of Christ, lay it down.

Jesus warns us that he'll show up wearing some distressing disguises (Matt 25:31–46). I don't want to laugh at him when he does.

Try This

- Take a trip to Walmart or its equivalent (grocery stores, malls, and non-membership "big box" stores also work). Find a bench by the checkout lines and just watch. Notice the diversity of the shoppers (gender, race, age, social status, languages spoken, etc.). What are people buying? Are any using coupons or food stamps? Are people alone or with others? What are the groupings like? How do people treat each other? What surprises you?

- Now consider—how does the clientele at Walmart compare with those who attend your church or are part of your friendship circle or your neighborhood? Whom do you see in the marketplace that's absent from those other spaces? Why might this be? Are there hidden prejudices, biases, or barriers that prevent or discourage those who are different from being part of your group? How can you change that?

13

Just Follow the Trash Trucks

Finding God at the Dump

Store your treasures in heaven, where moths and rust cannot destroy, and thieves do not break in and steal.

MATTHEW 6:20

WHO LOOKS FOR GOD on a pile of garbage?

Me . . . apparently.

A friend of mine was taking a load of old appliances to its final resting place at the town dump and invited me along. Cool, I thought, as I grabbed my camera. I'm going to look for God at the dump!

But right off the bat, I was shocked (and slightly disappointed) at how *nice* everything looked. No mounds of trash covered in flies, not even a hint of smell. We drove up an immaculately clean stretch of highway, past rolling hills covered in gently undulating native grass, to the entrance. Where were the requisite swarms of grackles and lines of vermin? Replaced by an exotic game ranch and an organic garden center.

Did I mention we were in Austin, Texas?

The city's innovative landfill even has a thrift shop provisioned with useful items pulled from your garbage. If you are trying to trash something that might sell, an aspiring sanitation worker will pluck it out, dust it off, and put a price tag on it. There, in an open-air flea market, are working

66

stereos, LPs, golf clubs, weights, clothing, elk heads, picture frames, medals, and mountains of stuffed animals (oh, the heartbreak).

It was sobering. Every one of these items had been trashed. I walked up and down aisles of junk, three thousand square feet of stuff people had thrown away. I ran my fingers over a flowered dress, a little toy train, and an electric guitar, trying to imagine the people who had chosen them, what they had paid to obtain them, the smile each item brought to someone's face. Birthday presents, new shoes, dreams. And yet . . . they all ended up at the dump: old, broken, out of date. Forgotten.

On about the fifth aisle, I found God . . . resting on a shelf between an old speaker and a Tupperware box. Dust coated a velvet cover that proclaimed: *Lifetime Memories*. Holding my breath, I opened the book, expecting photos yellowed with age, pictures of children and grandchildren. Instead, there were lines of signatures. First, a pastor, then family, friends. The "Houston Boys." Two people who wrote "sis" and "bro" beside their signatures. And at the very front, the name of the deceased. This poor soul's funeral book was thrown away, then picked out of the trash to resell.

"Someday," God whispered, "that will be you."

God met me in a pile of things that don't last to remind me of what does.

There is a type of wealth that vermin, decay, and time can't consume. There is a type of treasure that won't ever be thrown away. There is a type of investment that can't be sold at your estate sale. Jesus calls it "treasures in heaven" (Matt 6:20) and advises us to invest in these eternal riches.

How, though? It's not like they have an aisle for "heavenly treasures" in Target, Old Navy, or Walmart. How do we know what endures in a world where *everything* we're taught to value is headed to the dump?

I turned back to the abandoned funeral book. Its pages whispered the answer.

The first enduring treasure is that blank at the front of the book—the place for your name. The one thing you take to heaven is yourself.

Have you ever thought about who you want to be when you finish this race? When you are naked before God—without any of the stuff that surrounds you in life, without your phone, your home, your stocks—will you be happy with who you have become?

You determine how you cross that final finish line. True, there are things beyond your control. You don't get to opt out of tragedy or sorrow. You don't even get to know when your last day will come. But no matter what, you decide what to do with the hand you're dealt. You *are* in control of the person you are when you die.

Jesus says: Be light in a world of darkness, free your heart of anger, be forgiving, choose faithfulness over lust, keep your word, forgive those who don't deserve it, be generous, don't judge, pray with hope. Become, in short, the kind of people who are in short supply.

Grow your own soul into a garden instead of a vacant lot. I suspect many of us already know how this happens: pray, study your Bible, make time for worship, serve others. We know what needs to be done, but do we put our energy there? We won't become more generous or patient or courageous by accident. We must choose, and such choices require effort and sacrifice.

It makes me think of the most gifted pianist I've ever worked with. His name is Gustavo, and we worked together for ten years. Gustavo is an exceptional musician. Many members sit on the far left of the sanctuary just so they can watch his hands as he plays. Gustavo has natural talent, and he had excellent teachers. Yet it's so much more! Gustavo excels because for years and years he sat at the piano, playing, practicing, working. He didn't practice the violin, or listen to someone else playing, or just study music theory. Gustavo honed his skills by playing, hour after hour, day after day. He kept learning and pushing himself. Eventually, he began to teach piano to others, and that made him better still. Every year, he learns a little more. Gustavo plays music that lifts your spirit because that's what he's given his life to.

Let it be the same with your soul. Invest your time in growing closer to God. Your soul is one of the few things in this world that lasts, that you take with you into what comes next.

As I thumbed through that funeral book, I discovered the second thing that lasts: six full pages of family, friends, and loved ones. The names written there, "sis" and "bro" and a hundred others who came to this woman's funeral, are the second part of our heavenly treasure. The woman whose name was on the front page is gone, her possessions are in the dump, but these people remain. Her fingerprints, for good or bad, are all over their lives.

When you die, what will you have poured into others? What fingerprints will you leave on them? Jesus tells us that even the smallest acts of generosity, of time, of resources, of kindness, are noticed by God—a drink of water, a shared coat, a visit to someone captive to illness or poor choices (Matt 25:35–40). Every burden you lift is a treasure in heaven. Every time you help someone have faith or courage, you've built something eternal—something God notices.

This is not to say that having material possessions, or enjoying them, is bad. As I write this chapter, I'm snuggled under a colorful, soft blanket that my husband gave me. I love it! And I drag it all over the house on wintry days. But I try to remember that all I own, even this beautiful blanket, is transitional at best. Whereas doing one kind thing for another person—that lasts! Small things like phone calls, a meal, and kind words are the stuff of eternity.

My friend Amber was pregnant with her first child. She and her husband had been married a few years. They had a tiny house in the affordable part of town. He managed the town Game Stop; she was in grad school and working as a teacher's assistant.

The week before her due date, Amber went to Walmart for the essentials: diapers, wipes, baby bottles, a car seat, and some outfits. When the woman in line behind Amber saw her paying with food stamps, she stepped forward and quietly said she'd like to buy the non-WIC items, as a present.

Amber was shocked. She didn't know what to say, but it seemed like too much of a gift to accept from a stranger. The woman insisted. "I'd like to pay for this. It's my present to your baby. One day *you* will be able to help someone like this."

Stunned, almost speechless, Amber managed to stammer out a thank-you. She was so overwhelmed that she went to her car in a daze. But as she loaded up all those things the woman had purchased for her, Amber realized she wanted to say a deeper, more meaningful thank-you to this amazing woman. She looked all over the parking lot, then went back inside, eyes full of tears, scanning the store, hoping to see the kind lady. But the woman was gone.

That was years ago now. All the things bought that day have been used up. The little baby outfits have been outgrown—by two babies. But that day at the store endures in my friend's heart. She was changed because of that gift. And though she doesn't know the woman's name, she will never forget her. Amber wants to do for others what that stranger did for her.

Amber goes out of her way, looking for opportunities to show generosity and kindness. Amber and her husband give generously to those in need, far more than others whose income is much greater. She worked to create a park in her neighborhood, giving her time and expertise. A few years ago, she and that little girl, who was by then in middle school, drove to the Texas/Mexico border to visit, encourage, and support families with small children awaiting asylum hearings.

Do you remember what you bought fourteen years ago? Do you still have it? Amber remembers. Fourteen years ago, a stranger bought $100 worth of baby items, a gift that is still in Amber's heart to this day. And that lovely woman, even if she doesn't know it yet, has a beautiful treasure awaiting her in heaven.

Visit the dump and you'll see where the things we spend most of our lives acquiring end up. Everything—no exceptions. Don't waste your life on what's destined for the trash. Instead, pour your energy into the two treasures that endure: your soul and the lives of others.

Try This

- Visit the town dump. They often let you come on-site to drop off larger items. If you can, find a place to sit and look over all that has been discarded. Read Matt 6:19–21. Do you hear Jesus' teaching in a different way sitting in this space?

- Visit a thrift store. Walk through the aisles and ponder the discarded items. Pick up a couple and try to imagine what it felt like to buy them new, the hands that chose them, how it felt to bring them home. Sit in a chair or sofa that has been given away. Look around at all the stuff in that place. Then hear Jesus calling you to a purity of heart—to putting him above all possessions and the stuff of this world.

- Notice what you put into the trash this week. As you do, ponder the eternal "cousin" of that item. What eternal treasure comes to mind as you dispose of that which is used up on earth? How might you "store up" those unperishable things?

14

Stumps

How We Encounter God in Dry Times

Don't keep looking at my sins.
Remove the stain of my guilt.
Create in me a clean heart, O God.
Renew a loyal spirit within me.

PSALM 51:9–10

A FEW YEARS AGO, I looked out my office window at the Austin water supply, aka Lake Travis. The view from that office was glorious. At least when the lake was full—which it was when I arrived to pastor that community.

But a few short years into my ministry, Lake Travis looked like a bathtub being forcibly drained of water. We were in the teeth of the worst drought in sixty years. At one point, the lake was just 31 percent full. Officials warned we were as little as two years away from rock bottom.

Around the church, wells began to go dry, leaving families without water in their homes. The church, too, relied on well water. I wondered how many days we had until ours sputtered to a stop. You can purchase water and have it delivered, but for how long?

As the drought lengthened from months to years, the land baked and wildfires swept across the state. One of them tore through our community, swallowing forty-eight homes. I'll never forget holding hands with strangers and praying as we stood on the hill outside the church and watched another home catch fire.

During those years, most of us lived with two Rubbermaid containers filled with our most precious treasures, ready to grab if we had to evacuate. It's a strange thing to go through your home and pick the few things you want to save if the fire comes. Drought is more than inconvenient. Drought destroys lives. Drought robs you of safety.

We responded as you might imagine. We prayed. We lamented. We helped our neighbors rebuild. But as the drought continued, I watched the dryness seep into my people's consciousness. As the lake dried up, it took hope with it, drop by drop.

Drought changes the landscape, and not for the better. In the dry times, things the water once covered, surface. Mostly, it's trash, from debris as small as beer bottles and coke cans, to dumped items as large as refrigerators. One morning, I saw an old truck at the foot of a cliff I had driven by for years. The water slid back and there it was.

Who sank it there? And why? And how many decades ago was that? The ancient truck had been there all along but was only now visible. When the water seeps away, old bones come to the surface.

And what do we do? We pray like mad for rain to cover it all back up. Make it all disappear. But one night, as I drove home from one of those prayer meetings, I wondered . . . will we meet God only when the rain returns? Surely God was with us in the dry days too! But where? Where is God in the middle of the pain? Where is God in a drought?

My friend Max is a pastor with a lake house near College Station. Max's lake is one of the few that are considered "constant level." That lake, unlike so many in Texas, isn't anyone's drinking water. So its level shouldn't fluctuate like other lakes.

In college, we'd have leadership retreats at Max's lake house, alternating between planning sessions and water sports. When our work was done, the water beckoned. We'd catapult off the dock and into the water, surfacing with a burst of air and hauling ourselves back out, dripping and laughing, so we could do it again. Or, if Max was there, we'd convince him (it didn't take much) to pull out the boat. Some of us skied; others, like me, enjoyed the wild challenge of holding onto a giant inner tube while Max took turns fast enough to send us flying. I have lovely memories of that lake, the cool water, and the joy I shared with good friends.

But when my family and I paid Max a visit during the drought, I was shocked. That beloved place was unrecognizable. Max's dock now stood twenty feet above baked mud. There was no water to jump into, not for one hundred yards. And the lake? It now looked more like a draining swamp. Where a smooth surface once beckoned, acres of black barbs pierced the dark surface of the water. Stumps. Hundreds and hundreds of stumps.

We walked with Max to the end of his former dock and stood above the cracked dirt, the ruined lake. "Oh, I hope it rains" was all I could say.

"Not me," said Max.

Kevin and I chuckled darkly. Max was always good at gallows humor.

"No, really," said Max, "I hope it holds off. We have work to do." Max pointed at the stumps. He explained that those were the remains of an old forest that had been cleared to form the lake. The developers had done the bare minimum; they rhad emoved the trees, but hadn't cut the stumps low enough. Those stumps, Max said, had always been just below the surface. They had cost many a boat its propeller and wounded many a tuber. Without our knowing, Max had always kept the boat far away from the dangerous areas.

The homeowners all knew the problem, and though everyone wanted to fix it, they had discovered that doing so would involve an underwater dive team and specialized equipment: an astronomical cost. They couldn't begin to afford it. So they had done the only thing they could—they had lived with the occasional broken propeller and avoided the worst areas.

Then came the drought. While most in the neighborhood around the lake wrung their hands, a few like Max had had an idea. The stumps were finally *visible*. "We need to cut them down soon," Max said. "We can't wait, or the rain will come, and the lake will go back to normal. We will have lost our chance."

And there, in the middle of the drought, I met God.

Drought, painful as it was, provided an opportunity that was impossible in times of plenty. Drought gave that community the chance to *see* where the problems were and cut them out!

Isn't the same principle at work in our lives?

When you've had a good day, your energy is high, and you're well fed, I bet you're an amazing friend/spouse/parent/driver. But if it's a bad day, or the street is shut down, or your kids are sick, or someone quits to move to California, out of the depths rise those ugly stumps.

Drought reveals your stumps, forces you to see what the good times cover. It comes without permission: your job becomes unstable, your marriage hits the rocks, the stock market tanks, the world endures a deadly pandemic. Droughts as small as a stressful day or as large as the loss of someone we love hit, sucking away all that is good. Suddenly, ugly parts of your soul are exposed: anger, jealousy, over-indulgence, sharp words, lies, temptations. These stumps have always been there, below the surface, but the fat years hid them. In the drought, they are on display—the broken, awful parts of your character.

This happened to King David. After fifteen long years, David finally became king of Israel. His nation, *God's* nation, was secure. The battles that needed a warrior were won. The decisions that needed a king had been made. For David it was a lack of crisis, war, and division that brought a drought. In that lean time, an ugly part of his character surfaced: lust. David watched a woman bathe, then sent for her and slept with her. When he found out she was pregnant, he had her husband murdered to cover it up.

Over a year later, the truth came out. And when it did, David took a long, hard look at his soul. He had options. Kings made the laws, made the rules, and could punish those who spoke against them. David had already abused his power to cover up his sin. He could have tried to do so once more.

But David *didn't* try to cover up the painful sins that had come to light. David looked at those monstrosities and asked God to remove them from his soul. "Create in me a clean heart," he begs God (Ps 51:10). Blot out my sins. Renew my spirit. David isn't asking for water to cover up his sins. David's asking God to change the landscape of his heart! To help him cut the stumps out.

In Texas, drought makes beautiful landscapes ugly. Our blue lake drains away, leaving a nasty ring of trash, rot, and sunken vehicles. Each day the lake empties, it coughs up more debris. Each day, branches rise from the water's heart, dark and deadly. I hope and pray our leaders use this time to remove the dangers from our water supply. It's the droughts that give you a chance to see the stumps and address them.

But even more, I pray that when you face the droughts of life, you don't despair. It's good to pray for rain, but while you wait, use those low times to rid yourself of deadly stumps.

Try This

- Has your community experienced a disaster: A drought, flood, tornado, mudslide, earthquake, or fire? Some communities have a history of racial violence, financial crisis, or abuse of power by those in leadership. Most communities have trauma in their histories. Think of a spot that symbolizes that divide/loss/pain and go sit there. What was done to address those areas? Or were they covered up? Ask God what opportunity that sore place offers you, and your church, to see what is broken in your community.

- Find a neglected part of your home or yard. Maybe a fridge with moldy leftovers, a flower bed overrun by crab grass, a corner where things are piled, or an over-stuffed garage. Any place you wouldn't take a guest will do. As you sit in that space, ponder: What does the neglect of that area reflect? Does it show a need or lack in your life? Is it relational, emotional, functional, or even spiritual? As God makes that hurt visible, don't shy away. See it, name it, and ask for God's help to heal it.

15

Lucy in Disguise with Diamonds

God in a Costume Shop

The Kingdom of Heaven can be illustrated by the story of a man going on a long trip. He called together his servants and entrusted his money to them while he was gone.

MATTHEW 25:14

I LOOK AROUND: BATMAN, gorillas, steampunk, Renaissance knights, giant tacos . . . costumes from all genres fill every nook and cranny of Austin's famous "Lucy in Disguise with Diamonds." The store itself is a fun, funky space. It's huge—eight thousand square feet, I'm told—but so tightly packed that you have to burrow through it like a squirrel.

"Look," said my friend Linnea, pointing to the only truly visible thing—the ceiling. Each acoustic tile had been covered with a swatch of fabric in wild colors. "Is that wallpaper?" she wondered aloud.

From behind a display of jeweled necklaces, tiaras, and elbow-length gloves, a man seemed to rise as if by magic. He was dressed, head to toe, in tie-dye and wore prism glasses that made his eyes look like a psychedelic kaleidoscope. I'm not sure how he could see, but he gazed at the ceiling along with us. "Those tiles. Our owner, Jenna, decorated them like that when we opened in the eighties."

John, the prismatic hippie, went on to tell us about Jenna Radtke, founder and owner of Austin's landmark costume shop. From a very young age, Jenna Radtke had adored playing dress-up. But unlike others, she never outgrew her love of costumes. She was gifted at the art of pretend, and it brought her not only joy, but financial success. One Halloween in high school, Jenna made $9,000 by entering (and winning) every costume contest in town.

Costumes were Jenna's passion: a way to make friends, have fun, express herself. Jenna added to her growing collection every year, every *month*, until she had so many costumes that her friends staged an intervention. "You have too many," they soberly told her. "You either need to store the costumes or share them."

I found God in Austin's greatest costume shop when I learned that it all began with a choice: store it or share it. The same choice God gives every one of his children.

Jesus tells a story to help us understand this vital truth (Matt 25:14–30). He explains that being in God's family is like having a boss who trusts you to manage his valuable assets while he's away. What you get depends on your skill level, but everybody gets something. And the amounts are not insignificant. In today's dollars, each employee is given hundreds of thousands of dollars to invest. When the boss returns, two employees have put the resources to use. They return the money, doubled, and are commended. One man, though, has done nothing. He dug a hole and hid his money. He returns it in full, nothing more, nothing less. This man alone is condemned. He did nothing. Risked nothing. Tried nothing. He stored his treasure instead of sharing it.

God invites us to use our skills, our passions, and our own quirky giftings. Not to make money, but to make this world a bit more peaceful, whole, and hopeful. You are great at something. You love it. People come to you for advice about this thing. This is the million-dollar talent God has given you.

In that costume store, I was reminded that not all resources are seen on a bank statement. The owner had a skill and passion around costumes. And she faced a choice: keep it to herself or share it. In choosing to rent her beloved costumes, Jenna Radtke took a risk. The payoff was that she discovered a way to make a living that enriched her community. Lucy in Disguise is a beloved institution and a purveyor of fun (and weirdness) throughout the year.

There was another thing I was reminded of in that costume shop—the gifts God gives are not always overtly "religious" like preaching or teaching the Bible. Sometimes they are (I got one of those). But there is so much more! There are strategic gifts, like finance skills, organization, and construction. There are healing gifts, like bringing comfort, cooking, teaching, listening, or being a gifted doctor or nurse. There are dramatic gifts, like painting, cycling, flying helicopters, making music, and producing videos. In God's family, everyone has *something*.

A little over a year ago a nurse, a master gardener, and a retired engineer with a backhoe learned that children at the elementary school a few miles from our church didn't have enough to eat. Our food pantry worked to address food insecurity in our community, but provided only nonperishable staples. These children had no access to fresh fruits or vegetables. Candice, Clara, and Jim looked at the gifts God had given them—health care, gardening, and engineering—and chose to share those talents with their community. Today there is a garden next door to the elementary school that produces one hundred pounds of fruits, vegetables, and herbs every single month. God gave these believers gifts. They shared those gifts in a way that transformed the community. I can hear the joy as God proclaims, "Well done, my good and faithful servants!"

Hide it or share it.

Everybody has something.

I also remember the day a tall young man named Dan Schmidt approached me to say that he worked as an expert witness in lawsuits concerning construction failures. I was glad to know his skill set but hoped our church would never need it! Then Dan mentioned the building project the church was set to embark on: constructing a gym for the youth and children of our community. Dan offered to oversee the construction project, ensuring that none of the problems he'd seen would happen to us. Dan gave hours and hours of his expertise, every week. He interviewed architects and contractors. He reviewed contracts. He visited the construction site, sometimes daily. We could never have afforded an hour of Dan's time, but he gave hundreds. As a result, the children and youth of our community have a safe and welcoming space to play and learn.

Hide it or share it.

Everybody has something.

What has God given *you*? What will change in your community, in your church, in someone's life, when you share what God has given you?

The first step is to identify the gift God has given you. What do you love? What is something you're so good at that people ask your advice, look to you for help? Write down a few ideas and ask a few close friends for input. Pray. Then, once you have an idea—tell someone what you can do! Your pastor, the director of that nonprofit you love, a stressed-out teacher at the local elementary school. You may not know how or when God will need that skill, but just mentioning it to a pastor or friend is the first step.

Then, don't let fear hold you back. Jesus says it was fear that caused one person to hide his resources in the ground (Matt 25:25). I suspect he wasn't the only worker who was afraid. The other two just didn't let fear stop them. The workers who pushed through their fear end up with double what they'd started with. The only one who fails is the one who doesn't try.

I found God at Lucy in Disguise when I learned that the store started because someone told a woman whose talent lay in costumes that she either had to store them or share them.

If, thirty-five years ago, Jenna Radke had kept her costumes to herself, she would have made a killing each year at costume parties. But Austin would be so much less sparkly and fun.

We have a far better opportunity. We can offer our gift to God's kingdom and work to change the world. Everybody has something to share.

Try This

- What is your "superpower"? When do others seek you out for help? What ability does your employer value highly? What talent of yours are others always remarking on?

- To discover where God might have you invest your gift, fill out this little diagram. First, what gifts do you have? Next, what are you passionate about, interested in? Finally, where are the needs in your community? Passion + Gifts (without a true Need) is a hobby. Passion + Needs (without Gifting) will be frustrating. Gifts + Needs (without Passion) is a chore. But when you find the spot where they all meet, that's the place you can invest your gifts to change the world!

YOUR PASSIONS
YOUR GIFTS
YOUR CALLING
THE NEEDS

16

Farming Rabbits

God at a Livestock Auction

So those who are last now will be first then, and those who are first will be last.

MATTHEW 20:16

FUN FACT—I am a rabbit farmer.

Rabbit ranching took me by surprise. Yes, I am from Texas. But I did not grow up riding a horse, nor does my family own land or raise livestock. To be honest, I didn't even know rabbits could *be* livestock!

Then I was appointed to a country church in the hills outside of Austin. A member of my congregation, Dr. Matt, was the local veterinarian. Hearing of my daughter Leah's interest in veterinary medicine, Dr. Matt asked if she'd like to volunteer at his clinic on Saturday mornings. Leah, only eight years old, jumped at the chance. Each weekend, my elementary school kid shadowed her hero. She grabbed the tools he needed, met and talked to families, watched as he cared for animals large and small. Leah learned to draw up medicines and even observed minor surgeries. Oh, the joys of being a pastor's kid in a small community!

One day, Leah bounced out to the car to tell me that Dr. Matt had suggested she join 4-H. If she did, she could raise and show her own rabbits! Best of all, we could raise the rabbits in our backyard! Leah was all in. I was skeptical: Surely they didn't *really* let third-graders raise and show rabbits? Surely you had to be older? But my little girl was so excited that I promised to look into it. And if she was old enough, I said we'd figure it out. Well, she was. So we did.

For the past six years, starting in November when the baby rabbits arrive from the breeder, Leah gets up early to feed, water, and "work" her show rabbits. At night, she does it all again. There is a joke among parents that FFA (Future Farmers of America) really stands for "Fathers Feeding Animals." It's funny because it's true. Especially when the kids are young, parental help is crucial. But the quality of the help varies. And initially ours was watery, at best. My husband and I grew up in cities. We had no idea how to raise livestock at all, let alone rabbits.

I can now tell you, from experience, that show rabbits need to gain weight and muscle. To do so, they need water, food, a good living space, and lots of calm. They need an owner who will work their fur each day and handle them, so they get used to people. They need to be weighed and checked for health conditions, then treated for small problems that pop up (pink eye, ear mites, a cold). They need to be posed daily to learn how to hold still when the judge inspects them. In short, show rabbits need experienced care. If a rabbit gets so much as a broken *toenail*, it is disqualified from competition.

Here's a small list of things *not* to do with your show rabbits:

- Make an obstacle course in the front yard for them to "enjoy."
- Put them in your purse and take them on "adventures."
- Introduce them to your neighbors.
- Introduce them to your dog.
- Introduce them to your baby brother.
- Bring them inside to watch TV.
- Snuggle them in your loft bed.
- Take them down the slide on your friend's playset.
- Put them in a bucket tied to a rope so they can see the top of your friend's tree house.

The first year Leah showed rabbits, her bunnies experienced all these delights . . . and more. In the middle of this seemingly doomed process, a church friend who actually had a background in 4-H and FFA visited our house. Derik observed the bunny obstacle course in action. After asking

Kevin and me a few questions (and finding us woefully lacking), Derik turned to our eight-year-old and addressed her directly.

"Leah," he said, "what's your goal with these rabbits? Do you want to win the competition? Or do you just want to have fun?"

"I'd just like to have fun," she said. "I know I won't win."

"Good," he said. "If fun is your goal, you're doing great. If you want to get more serious, there is always next year."

And that was that.

The day of the show, our friend Derik came with us to support Leah in her first competition. Leah stood in line with 150 students from all over the county to check in her rabbits. Unlike Leah, most of the other competitors were in high school. It took almost an hour before Leah reached the rabbit judge for the weigh-in. She kept her hands clasped behind her back, a little girl in a plaid shirt and braids. The judge expertly flipped and measured her pen (group of three rabbits), making some quick notes on an index card. Then Leah was asked to move her rabbits' cage to the sawdust floor of the arena with the other competitors' pens.

As we waited for the remaining pens to be evaluated, Derik explained that once the judge was done weighing and examining the rabbits, he would take a quick break, then begin to call all the competitors back into the ring. In this competition, Derik said, you wanted your number to be called last. The first competitors invited back into the ring were the worst. They would be the first to be "culled" from the group.

Well, we were all ready to hear Leah's pen number in the first group. But amazingly, Leah's rabbits were not in the first cull! This was a surprise, a shock even. Leah giggled with joy. The second group was called, and still, Leah's rabbits were in the running.

"It's incredible . . . she just might have a shot!" Derik whispered to me under his breath. We could hardly believe it.

Incredibly, Leah made it to the final group of forty (it turns out having a good breeder can go a *very* long way). As competitors in this group were dismissed, one by one, Leah and her bunnies remained. Our tiny third-grader stood ramrod straight and kept her eyes on the judge. She was surrounded by high school students, a little girl in a crowd of giants.

A hush fell over the spectators. Derik leaned in. "They are about to start giving ribbons. And if you get one, you have a shot at going to auction."

I have never cheered so loudly for twenty-fifth place in my life! We were high-fiving and taking pictures and making such a commotion, you would have thought we'd won Grand Champion. The veterinarian, Dr. Matt, was so excited for Leah that he took a picture with her, the ribbon, and her favorite rabbit, Lumpy. He's still got it framed in his lobby. Twenty-fifth place! A huge, unexpected moment of grace. We had made the auction!

Later that week, we drove an hour and a half to the other side of the county, arriving at 10 a.m., when the livestock auction started. Nobody had told us that rabbits were going last. Experienced rabbit wranglers strolled in around 3 p.m. But we were brand-new and had no clue. So, we just waited and watched the auctions of all the other species: steer, sheep, goats, pigs, turkeys, and chickens. Finally, at 5 p.m., it was the rabbits' turn.

But that was also when bidders started to drift off. The room filled with the sound of chairs folding together and table legs being snapped into storage position. People gathered their belongings to go. Please, I prayed. Please stay a little longer. Please stay for my little girl.

Thankfully, a few did. And thankfully, Leah didn't pick up on the crowd's waning interest. Her eyes popped when the final amount was called out for her rabbits, and she bounced off stage to go thank her buyer.

There was only one kid after her. One last auction item—the boy with the twenty-sixth-place pen of rabbits. Last to qualify, last in importance. The bottom of the bottom. Trevor, another boy in Leah's 4-H, took the stage. And something amazing happened: the bidding got high. I mean *really* high.

Trevor raised the last-place rabbit pen. But the buyers were so enthusiastic that the auctioneer eventually had to stop them. This final pen was going to earn more than the Reserve Grand Champion! They couldn't allow that—bidding was cut off. The Reserve Grand Champion and the twenty-sixth-place finisher got the same amount—*thousands* of dollars!

I was confused and, honestly, a bit miffed. This did not seem at all fair. Watching my face, another mom with lots of experience leaned over to explain. "He's last. It's *always* amazing to be last. These corporations know how much they want to give away. At the end of the day, if any of them still have leftover money, they put it all on the very last animal, whoever that is."

Sitting there, pondering that last-minute generosity, I found God at the livestock auction. As Trevor bounced off the stage with delight, I heard *and felt* Jesus' words: "So the last will be first, and the first will be last" (Matt 20:16).

When did Jesus say that? Well, he was telling a story (Matt 20:1–16). A story about a man who owned a vineyard and needed workers to bring in the crop.

As the sun rises, the landowner, who represents God, goes into town to hire workers. They agree on a daily wage and the workers start the harvest. Throughout the day, the owner returns to town and, seeing more people waiting for work, hires them. No set amount is given. They are late to the party, so he promises to pay only "whatever [is] right" (Matt 20:4). These late workers must rely on the landowner's goodness. They are happy to have the work, happy to be able to provide *something* for their families.

Back then, the final hour of the workday was called the eleventh hour. The eleventh hour is the time just before sunset when the work is wrapping up and everyone is about to head home. Unbelievably, the eleventh hour rolls around, and a new group drags themselves out to look for work. I can't imagine how troubled their lives were if they finally start to look for work at 5 p.m. But the owner sees and hires them. A price isn't even discussed. They are in no position to bargain.

Although none of the late workers knows what they are going to earn, the owner has already decided to pay every single one a full day's wage. The landowner knows that every additional person he picks up, especially so late in the day, is a financial drain. But that doesn't stop him. There is always room for one more.

What does it mean to be part of God's family, part of God's reign on this earth? Well, it's like a landowner who will hire you no matter when you arrive. And who will treat you the same, no matter when you got there. You won't get a small portion of love, with the fullest reserved for those who have been with God the longest. Everyone gets the full amount.

And the price? Well, it's the same for everyone. Jesus paid it when he died for you. No matter when you take him up on that offer, he paid for you with his life.

What I saw that day at the livestock auction reminded me of the heart of Jesus' teaching: last place can be first place with God. There aren't rankings in faith like in life. There aren't favorites. People who joined God's family when they were six are just as welcome and valuable as those who joined at seventy-six.

But if I'm being completely honest, that day at the livestock auction helped me understand something else about Jesus' story—the emotions felt by the first workers. The people hired at dawn are indignant. This is not fair! Those latecomers did one-tenth of the work, but still got the same pay!

In the livestock auction that day, I knew how those first workers felt. It stung when generosity was poured out on another, lower down the line. I kept thinking: Those donors should spread their giving out! Maybe bless the *second-to-last* kid too.

But I found God in Leah's response.

Leah didn't share my jealousy. She ran over to me and gave me the biggest hug.

"Mom, can you believe how much I made? We weren't even supposed to be here! Next year, I can buy my own rabbits and get them new cages. You and Dad don't have to spend your money. Mom, I am so excited."

Leah wasn't comparing herself to anybody else. She was overjoyed by what the donors had bid for *her* rabbits—more money than she'd ever had! And it came to her as a complete gift from strangers who wanted to encourage and support her.

Leah's grateful spirit also allowed her to celebrate something else. Leah was happy for Trevor without feeling like his good fortune took anything from her own. "Mom," she said, "I know him! That boy who went last. Do you recognize him? That's Trevor from my 4-H. I bet he's so excited! As much as the Reserve Grand Champion! I'm going to go give him a hug."

I found God at the livestock auction. In the boy who came last—lowest animal, worst pen of all. I saw God's generosity in the donors who wanted to help a child realize his dreams, even at the eleventh hour. And I found God in my daughter's response: she focused on the kindness she received and celebrated *all* the day's blessings, even when they fell to others.

The offer that God makes, equally to all of us, is that no matter when we ask for a fresh start, it's never too late. No matter when you come, you'll be treated like you've always belonged. Because you always have. With God, everyone is a Grand Champion.

Try This

- Find a vineyard, orchard, or even a little garden plot or flower bed where things have been planted and tended with care. Look at that space and consider how Jesus compares God to a farmer and us to workers in God's fields. What does it mean to work in someone else's garden? Think about the ways you "work" for God throughout the day and ways you could be more fully employed for God.

- Find ways to move others forward this week. Allow people to go in front of you in line. Pay for a stranger's meal or coffee. Let other drivers, even the abhorrent "side-zoomers," merge in front of you. As you do, notice what it feels like to choose to serve instead of grabbing the best for yourself.

17

Fireflies

Finding God in Second Chances

One day Moses was tending the flock of his father-in-law, Jethro, the priest of Midian. He led the flock far into the wilderness and came to Sinai, the mountain of God. There the angel of the Lord appeared to him in a blazing fire from the middle of a bush. Moses stared in amazement. Though the bush was engulfed in flames, it didn't burn up. "This is amazing," Moses said to himself. "Why isn't that bush burning up? I must go see it."

EXODUS 3:1–3

A COMMON REGRET OF the dying is how they used their time. Many give voice to a similar lament: they wish that they'd spent more time on the important things and less on stuff that didn't matter.

You don't have to be dying to regret how you've spent your days. I also lament my use of time. Too often, I've rushed past the beauty God sets before me, unable or unwilling to stop trivial tasks that seem all-consuming. As a result, I have missed experiences that I can never recover.

One of these moments stands out, a symbol of all the rest. It happened more than twenty years ago. Kevin and I were visiting his family in Kansas for the first time. I was anxious to impress everyone. Although we weren't yet engaged, we were talking about getting married. These folks would someday be my family.

A couple of years before, Kevin had broken up with his longtime girl-friend. I knew his family still silently (and not-so-silently) preferred her to me. Heck, his grandma still had her picture on the mantel! I desperately wanted my future in-laws to like me, to approve. That evening the whole family was to gather at an aunt's house in the country. These were German farmers, and dinner was at 6 p.m. sharp.

The sun was setting as Kevin drove us through the Kansas hills to the place where the plains opened up and farming began. The road took us through fields of ripening corn. Then, as we turned a corner, I gasped. Fireflies. A whole cornfield *full* of fireflies. Not just one or two, like I'd seen when I was a kid in San Antonio, but hundreds, *thousands* of fireflies, danc-ing and flickering in the twilight of a Kansas summer. It was like visual music. A canvas of lights calling us to stop and rejoice in a God who created such beauty, a fiery show to welcome in the gathering dusk.

God whispered to Moses from a burning bush. And Moses, seeing it, left the tasks of the day, left his sheep, and drew near.

When I saw those fireflies burning in the late summer twilight, I longed to linger and listen to the whisper of God. We even stopped the car to marvel: One breath. Two. Oh, to stay longer . . . but the third breath came. And I listened to a different voice. People were waiting: expectations and deadlines and responsibilities in a farmhouse ten miles away. I wanted to impress those people. "We are going to be late," I said.

To my great sorrow, I turned us away from the beauty, the whisper of God. I chose to leave one of the most luminous sights I've ever encountered to attend a dinner I don't even remember. I left a place where heaven and earth were thin because I felt guilty stopping to take it in. A burning bush, God's whisper, and I was too busy tending my sheep.

Those fireflies have come to symbolize for me all the times I've cho-sen poorly, putting my schedule, a meeting, or a project ahead of my kids, my husband, or spending time with God. The night I missed the fireflies reminds me of all the times I've let the business of life distract me from the beauty of it.

The best I've been able to do by way of atonement is to learn from that missed chance. To learn to respond when God whispers. Because moments like that don't come again. Believe me, I've been hoping to see something like that again for more than twenty years now. Sometimes I tell Kevin we should go to Kansas to see his family. But he and I both know it's also because I'd like to see if we could find a firefly field again. He gently reminds me that the moment is gone. We missed it.

And then, in my tenth year of ministry, my amazing church gave me a sabbatical. It was time, they said, to step away and renew. To tend to my own soul instead of the souls of hundreds.

I had gotten a grant and planned an amazing schedule of learning, rest, and adventure. But out of all those many months, the adventures, the difficulties, the delights, I remember the first day the best. The day when I stopped working and began to rest. Nothing special, but everything special. A bagel with my husband as he went to work. Prayer time in my chair—and lingering to watch birds in the garden. Picking up kids from school. That night, Kevin and I took a walk around our neighborhood at twilight. We came over a hill we'd walked hundreds of times and down into the valley below. There, dancing in a grove of oak trees just behind our house, were hundreds of fireflies.

I sat down.

I marveled.

I watched the fireflies dance.

And thanked God, from the bottom of my heart, for second chances.

I expected to be renewed on my sabbatical. I didn't expect to be healed. Sometimes, God really does let us do it all over again. And this time, we get it right.

God is everywhere around us. Everywhere. Bushes are burning. Fireflies are dancing. God is whispering to our aching hearts a song of love. I want you to hear, to notice, to stop and soak it in. Because there are places all over this world where the space between heaven and earth is thin. So thin.

If I could give you a gift, it would be this: I give you permission to stop when you hear God whispering. Moses left the sheep alone on a mountainside to look at that burning bush. It changed his life. It changed the lives of thousands of others. Right down to you and me.

Even if it's a bad time, stop. Sit down. Take it in. Enjoy your own firefly moments. Those times when the space between heaven and earth is thin. And God whispers your name.

Try This

- What restores your soul? What activities, hobbies, events, places, or people invariably pour energy, rest, hope, healing, or restoration into you? Perhaps you love to draw, or run, or sing, or swim. Maybe you love being outside in the yard, fishing, reading, or welding. Make a list of "firefly" moments from your past so you can pay attention when they pop up next.

- This week—don't just notice "firefly" events; stop to appreciate them. For one week, even if you are running late, take time to watch the sunset, the dog chasing bugs across the yard, the baby laughing, the kids playing sports. What tugs at your heart; what fills up your soul? This week, give space and attention to those things when they pop up. Then notice corresponding increases in thankfulness, joy, and peace.

- What regrets do you carry from times you were too busy to stop for something important? Bring that sorrow to God. Ask for a second, third, or fiftieth chance. If there is someone your distraction or busyness has hurt, seek their forgiveness. Then get out there and be fully awake to all the things worth stopping for.

18

Throwing Axes . . . with the Bishop

When God Speaks through Failure

We are the clay, and you are the potter.
We all are formed by your hand.

ISAIAH 64:8

THROWING AXES IS A GREAT way to learn how to lead a church.

Right?

Sure.

That's what four other pastors and I decided. We're part of a little learning cohort. Our goal: to get outside our comfort zones, try new things, and learn to accept and overcome challenges. We want to do weird stuff that will help us grow and strengthen our leadership. So, axe throwing . . . *obviously!*

Only we discovered that learning to throw axes required a minimum group of six people. We needed one more sucker . . . I mean, *participant.* I had a brainstorm—let's invite our bishop!

I'm a United Methodist pastor, which is kind of like being in the military, in that I don't find my own church. Our bishop oversees hundreds of churches in a general area (mine is the central and southern part of Texas). The bishop looks at all the churches, and then at all the pastors, and makes a call to ask (tell) us where to go.

93

Inviting the bishop to throw axes might not have been my best idea. In my defense, though, I didn't think he'd *agree*. Axe throwing seems very un-bishopy, and I gave him a nice out. But the bishop called my bluff. He immediately told me he'd love to join us—when and where?

So there I was, one cold January day in Austin, in a dirt parking lot with potholes the size of a Prius, waiting for the bishop to arrive so we could all learn to throw axes together. Unfortunately, one of the doors of a parked SUV opened and out came the bishop. He'd beaten me there. I'd kept him waiting in a sleezy parking lot in the dodgy part of town.

"Which way?" the bishop asked. I had no clue, but I tried to exude confidence as I walked to the door at the front of the metal building. It was boarded shut, the handles wrapped in a chain. I groaned inside. The bishop turned to look at me. "Do you know what you're doing?" he asked. Ugh. I had not anticipated that my first learning experience would be to just find the dang entrance.

I managed it. The door was around the back of the building by, I kid you not, a trash can fire. I have no idea what the bishop thought of that, but I quickly hustled us both inside, just glad to be somewhere that looked more official. There was a long sales counter and some stands where you could sign waivers on iPads. "Am I really agreeing to my possible death?" the bishop asked me as we initialed the many disclaimers. "Ha. Ha!" I said. Although I'm not sure he was joking.

At the desk, they giddily told me that my group was in luck! Today was the Urban Axes *staff party*. We'd be surrounded by axe-throwing masters. They hadn't mentioned that little tidbit when we'd booked the date.

One of the staff broke away from the party and guided our group to a couple of lanes in the center of the celebration. She went over safety, made a couple of off-color axe jokes, and pulled out a bucket of axes. "Who's first?" There was a pregnant pause, then the group pushed me to the front.

Jerks . . . (but not you, bishop).

Okay, I told myself. This is going to be *fun*. I'm going to throw bullseyes. There will be photos and videos and I will look so cool and hip: an axe-throwing pastor!

My first throw, though, was . . . *impressively awful*. And loud. It hit the ceiling, then ricocheted off the metal cages surrounding the lane, then bounced off the rubber padding to clatter around on the concrete floor. Dozens of bearded and flannelled staff paused their celebrations to look.

I fast-walked to grab my axe, trying to laugh it off, while blushing bright pink.

I was bad at throwing axes.

Really bad.

Noisily bad.

So bad, my friends laughed. The staff laughed. The bishop laughed.

It flat-out stinks to be publicly terrible at something you are trying your best to nail.

That was my second unexpected challenge—to get comfortable with unrelenting failure. Thomas Edison kept running through my head. When asked about how often he failed on the way to the lightbulb he responded, "I didn't fail a thousand times. The light bulb was an invention with one thousand steps." But honestly, would axe-throwing be one thousand steps? I sincerely hoped not. I didn't know if I had it in me.

Mercifully, my "practice turn" ended, and I got to retreat to the high table behind the throwing area where everyone else sat. I beelined for one of the bottles of wine the pastors brought and poured a healthy cup. Yes, I knew the bishop would see me imbibing, but y'all, I needed a drink. A drink . . . and the chance to see how bad everyone else was. That would hit the spot.

Only, darn it, they succeeded with only a few throws. I just wanted one person to be as bad as me. Just one. But they all learned faster, threw better, and were having a lot more fun. I sipped more wine.

Once everyone had practiced, Melody, the instructor, surveyed the group and asked, "So, who's ready for the tournament . . . or do we need more practice?" She was looking at me when she said that last bit. Part of me wanted to get this excruciating learning experience over with. But maybe just a few more test throws and I'd get better too?

"Practice," I said quickly. All the other pastors graciously agreed. This time, we went in pairs. I was partnered with my buddy Jay, who (*punk*) had not only managed to hit the target, but was now throwing *one-handed*. Show-off. I took a breath. I focused on the target. I held the axe as they had told me.

Jay threw . . . *bullseye!*

I threw . . . *clang*.

Jay and I went to retrieve our axes. The instructor gave me her undivided attention. "Hmm," she said. "Do you know jazz hands? Yes? Finish down here with jazz hands." She put her hands by her sides, but back a little, fingers flared. It seemed silly.

But so did failure.

Sighing, I tried the jazz hands follow-through. The axe stuck. It *stuck*! My friends cheered! The bishop cheered! Pictures were taken! I breathed a sigh of joyful relief.

Then I had to throw again. And once again, I was terrible. The instructor returned. "Think of the Little Mermaid. Be like the Little Mermaid on that rock. Throw your head up, chest out, hands down." If jazz hands were mildly embarrassing, this was *utterly* ridiculous. Especially with the bishop watching.

But wasn't failure worse? So, I tried to be the Little Mermaid on a rock. Bullseye!

I hit the *bullseye*!

I sure hoped someone got it on video . . .

I was right that throwing axes would help me become a better leader. But it was a much more painful and much less cool lesson than I'd expected. The Christian life feels a lot like that experience to me. God continually invites us into new challenging spaces: to learn, grow, become better followers. God delights in using the least likely folks to do the most amazing things. "You're up!" God has told generations of unexpected people. In a sea of experts, God picks ordinary people like you and me. But to succeed, we must listen to God's guidance.

Just think of Jesus' followers! Jesus calls grown men (and women, I'd argue) away from all they knew, out of professions they were good at, and into territory where all became novices again. A few disciples knew all about fishing, another about collecting taxes, but none of them knew anything about healing blind eyes, or teaching people about God, or feeding the hungry. To succeed, the disciples had to let Jesus *teach* them. They had to be pliable, moldable, supple clay in God's hands. They failed a lot. But those with teachable hearts were ultimately transformed into the amazing leaders we look up to today.

A good example comes from comparing two of the disciples: Judas and Peter. These men's stories end in radically different ways. And yet, if you put the ending aside for a moment, there are some unsettling similarities:

- Jesus chooses both men.

- Both men experience setbacks and failures.

- Jesus recognizes evil in both, calling Peter "Satan" (Matt 16:23) and Judas "a devil" (John 6:70).

- Jesus rebukes both—Peter when he balks at Jesus' need to die and Judas when he accuses Mary of wasting perfume.

- Both men betray Jesus: Judas for a handful of silver, Peter out of fear.

  Yet Judas became the Betrayer.
  While Peter became the Rock.

The difference? Peter was willing to learn. When he was rebuked, Peter sought to do better. When he failed, Peter tried to understand so he could change. When he denied Christ, Peter was eager to be forgiven.

Judas never allowed his heart to be changed. He was unwilling to grow. Unwilling to learn from the great Teacher.

Being a follower of Jesus means you will be forever growing and improving. The minute your pride tells you to stop listening, or that you already know this, or you're too good for this idiocy, you're done. You are stuck right where you are.

Throwing axes was a great way to grow as a leader—just not in the way I expected. That experience reminded me that Jesus doesn't expect perfection from his followers. He knows we won't always hit a bullseye, or even the target. But Jesus asks us to keep listening to his voice, keep letting his hands shape us.

That's a bullseye every time.

Try This

- Try something you know you'll be bad at. Rent or borrow a game console and attempt to play a popular video game. Fly a drone. Throw some pottery. Try improv. How does it go? How does it feel? Notice the attitude you need to learn. Notice your feelings around failing.

Use this experience to remind yourself to meet God in moments of struggle, when you confront your limitations and failings.

- Think of someone in an ordinary profession who made or makes a difference in your life. Take some time to thank them for their contribution. God calls most of us, not to greatness, but to being faithful in the daily choices of life.

19

Teen Driving

How Hard Can It Be?

You have heard me teach things that have been confirmed by many reliable witnesses. Now teach these truths to other trustworthy people who will be able to pass them on to others.

2 TIMOTHY 2:2

"Why don't you look for God in a teen driving school?"

Some sadist suggested this a couple of years ago. "Or, better yet," he added with a wicked glint in his eye, "look for God while riding with a teen driver!" I tried, but for liability reasons (go figure), the local driving school was unable to let me ride with their students. I sat in a few classes, but those experiences didn't capture the life-or-death terror this man imagined. Thus, I bided my time and grew my own teen driver.

My suspicion, though, was that our eldest, Anna, would fail to meet the requirements of this man's request. She, I firmly believed, would defy conventional teen-driving stereotypes. There would be no fear, no terror. Driving with Anna would be only joy and peace.

I was more than a little naïve about this. And yes . . . more than a little smug. You see, a couple of years before, my husband Kevin and I had bought a beat-up old golf cart. And by beat-up, I mean it rolled off the line in 1981. We named it "The Little Engine That Could" and used it to zip around our spread-out country neighborhood. I say zip . . . The Little

Engine was so slow going up hills that we often got out and walked beside it, just to lighten its burden (and because walking was faster!). But going downhill the Little Engine broke the sound barrier. Our ancient golf cart was manufactured in a day before governor switches. That baby could fly.

The Little Engine felt like a stroke of parental genius. Not only could we zip around the neighborhood, we could use it to teach the girls to drive! First, they sat at our side. Then, we let them practice on the neighborhood golf course, after hours. The girls worked their way up: puttering down our quiet cul-de-sac before being allowed to drive down to the park, or to the marina, or to a friend's house. Kevin and I taught them the rules of the road, how to look both ways, where the gas and brake were, even how to check the rearview mirror. Anna got so good that we trusted her to drive the golf cart alone to babysit in the neighborhood, and parents let their kids ride with her.

With this ingenious golf cart preparation, I had no doubt Anna was going to crush it at driving a real car. My child would be the best teenage driver ever—defying all stereotypes. After all, isn't an SUV just a golf cart writ large? (Oh, I was so naïve!)

I decided to look for God the first time Anna got behind the wheel of a real car. But I wondered if I'd notice anything. Remember—she was going to be *amazing*. Maybe, I reasoned, I would discover God in the utter peace and satisfaction of a job well done?

I had no fear as I handed Anna the keys to my SUV. My husband and I both thought driving would be a wonderful treat. We took Anna to eat tacos, then surprised her with the offer of driving my car around the deserted parking lot behind the shopping center. She was giddy. I was giddy. "Film this," I told Kevin, "so we can always remember."

That film will never see the light of day. Anna has forbidden it. The night Anna moved from golf cart to SUV, angels did not sing. The sun did not break through the clouds to shine on her. Officers didn't appear to give her awards and shake her hand. But there were tears. And I did discover God . . . just not where I had expected.

Picture, if you will, a lovely spring evening in central Texas. The sun was starting to sink in the sky as I backed the car out of its parking place and pulled it around back. It was so beautiful outside that I rolled down all the windows to savor the sweet twilight breeze.

I stopped in the lane of a semi-full parking area. Anna would need to drive down that car-lined aisle, make a left, then turn right to reach the deserted area. She could do it. No problem.

Anna got in and adjusted the seat. Put it in drive like an ace. Drove carefully between the parked cars. Made a smoothish left turn. And approached her first-ever stop sign.

That's when the wheels came off. Not literally, thank God. But in most every other sense of the word. Anna needed to stop. But for some reason, she wasn't stopping. Maybe she just hadn't seen?

"Stop, Anna," I said, casually, a tiny edge to my voice. She could do this simple thing. I mean, she drove the golf cart. The pedals are *the same*. The signage is *the same*.

But Anna wasn't stopping.

"Mom . . ." she said . . . voice slightly raised. "How?"

Oh, no! I hadn't planned for this. And me, a pastor who loves words, who uses them every day to instruct, guide, comfort, and convince, couldn't utter a single one of them.

All I had to say was: "The pedal on the left—the brake." That's the instruction my child so desperately needed. But I couldn't speak. Couldn't think. I was completely useless. Just when my daughter needed me most.

Anna later explained to us what happened: in the golf cart she could always see both pedals. As she pulled up to the stop sign, she became unsure. When she looked to check and couldn't see her feet, she panicked.

But it gets worse. As Anna slowly rolled up on that stop sign, I saw another car coming along the main (typically deserted) route. Anna *had* to stop. The other car had the right-of-way. We were going to be T-boned. Even then, all I could manage to give my child in terms of help was to repeat the action she needed to take: "Stop! Anna! *Stop!*"

Sadly, it wasn't the *instruction* Anna was missing. It was the *how-to*. Anna hit the blinker. She hit the windshield wipers. "Mom," she squeaked, "help!"

I tried the invisible pedal on my side of the car. Nope. We rolled through the stop sign. Even if we weren't T-boned, Anna was going to crash the SUV through the wooden end-of-road barrier across from us and plunge the car down into the ravine on the other side. From the backseat, my husband yelled yet another loud, useless instruction: "Stop the car!" (What a pair we are!) I clutched the armrest and braced for impact.

Miraculously, Anna found the brakes. All on her own. The car came to a stop two-thirds of the way through the intersection and a few feet from the end-of-road barrier. The car that was about to hit us also found their brakes in time and screeched to a halt a foot from my passenger door.

We sat there, wide-eyed and terrified as our car's wipers flashed back and forth and the turn signal clicked on and off. I didn't want to look at the other driver. Making eye contact would cement what had just happened. But I had to own it, so I slowly turned my head to the right, to the car that had almost hit us (and wouldn't have been at fault if it had!). Six feet away from me, the other driver wore an equally shocked expression. She collected herself and waved Anna on, mouthing the words, "Go ahead, sweetie." What a lovely, kind woman. I widened my eyes even further and shook my head at her. "Oh, no. Go around us. *Please.*"

I found God as I sat in that intersection, dumbstruck and sweating, and my daughter began to cry. I found God in the need to be a teacher, a *much* better teacher than I had just been.

The state trusts us to teach our teens to drive.

God trusts us to teach *the faith* to other people.

(And to do more than just scream, "Stop, stop, *stop!!*")

First, we learn the faith. Then we teach the faith. It's what God calls us to do. *All* of us. Teaching others about God isn't something God wants us to leave to "the experts," people with advanced degrees or those who have read the Bible cover-to-cover dozens of times. Teaching others about God is much more democratic, like teaching people to drive. It's something *every* believer is expected and trusted to do.

Jesus trusts ordinary people with carrying the good news to the entire world. Think of the first disciples. We tend to imagine these men as they ended up: saints immortalized in stained glass windows, holy and utterly other.

And yet, when Jesus calls them, they are ordinary. The disciples' education would have included Torah school; it's something all Jewish boys did, like Sunday school. Everyone in that day reached a certain basic level. Those who were incredibly gifted moved on. If they kept moving upward, they could become rabbis, scribes, or religious scholars. Those who didn't have what it took (most of the population) finished the basics and went on to practice a trade or learn a vocation.

When Jesus prays about who will become the foundation of the new covenant community, none of the recruits come from the scholarly ranks. Jesus doesn't pick people who achieved the highest levels of Bible and religious knowledge. Jesus calls people who know the basics, everyday people like you. Jesus trusts ordinary people to carry on his teaching.

We are here because those first disciples answered Jesus' call. They allowed the Holy Spirit to work in and through them. They taught dozens, then hundreds, then thousands of people what it meant to follow Jesus. The faith spread from town to town and then country to country. People with a very basic Scripture education, a very deep time with Jesus, and a profound trust of the Holy Spirit, became the foundation of the church.

But the work still isn't finished. Still today, Jesus calls ordinary followers like you to go out in his name and help people know they have a Savior who loves them, who sets them free.

The faith has always been about folks like *you*. People who haven't spent three years in seminary. People who have what they learned in Sunday school, or in their devotional times, or maybe a Bible study. Jesus trusts *you* to share what you know about him with the next person. Our amazing God calls you to share your faith; empowers you to do it!

I know it seems scary sometimes . . . as scary as getting in the car with a teenage driver. But the only way the next generation will know our Savior is if all of God's "ordinary people" take a big deep breath, sit down in the passenger seat, brace themselves, and *try*.

First, we learn. Then we teach. God trusts *you* with teaching the faith to people of all ages. You can do it. You are exactly who God needs. So buckle up, church. It's up to us to teach others about our amazing Savior.

And let's make sure those seat belts are extra tight because we're about to move out another ring. Next up is Jesus' call to Samaria, where we will be stretched way beyond our comfort zone. The call to Samaria challenges us to meet God in places and with people who might be geographically close but are culturally, morally, or spiritually very different.

Try This

- Sign up for a class on something you'd like to learn. Observe the teacher and how they relate with you, with the other students. Apart from expertise, what are some of the traits you most value in them?

- Talk with someone about your faith story. Don't stress or overthink it. Just find a chance to tell someone this week something God has been doing in your life. This doesn't need to be memorized or cheesy. You don't have to quote Scripture. Just try sharing the story of God's work in your life. Notice what happens, how it feels. What was good in that experience? What was scary?

SAMARIA
Meeting God in Foreign Territory

20

Hulk Smash

Of Prophets and Demolition Derbies

On the day Jonah entered the city, he shouted to the crowds: "Forty days from now Nineveh will be destroyed!"

JONAH 3:4

ONE OF MY FAVORITE things about being appointed to a new community is discovering each town's special events. You can tell a lot about a community by what they celebrate. In San Angelo, the biggest events were the Fourth of July and the rodeo. In New Braunfels, the county fair and Wurstfest. In Spicewood, though, the big event was the demolition derby.

The derby is the Spicewood Volunteer Fire Department's major fundraiser. It draws a crowd, and not a "churchy" one. Before I went there to look for God, I asked a few locals to explain the rules. Here are a few fun facts:

- Cars do not drive straight at each other, but always hit in reverse because it protects the engine.

- A car must contact (read, smash into) another car in the ring within two minutes or it is disqualified.

- There is no hitting the driver's side door, on which is painted a big *x*.

- The Chrysler Imperial is banned because it's so dang well built that it creates an unfair advantage.

- The derby is typically held outside, in August, in the scorching afternoon sun.

Looking for God has never been for the faint of heart. And this time, the whole family wanted to come. We arrived early (it gets very crowded) and found our way to empty places on the stands that had been set up all around the derby arena. We positioned dish towels and rags on the scorching metal bleachers (thank God for helpful locals who shared this life-hack) and sat down. As we waited for the crunching to begin, I snuck glances at the folks around me.

The derby is a BYOB event, and a large percentage of the crowd had apparently gotten an early start. I watched a seven-year-old take drink orders and distribute the appropriate cans and bottles from a large cooler. A beefy drunken biker stood right in front of me on several occasions, which really should be where I found God, because he blocked the sun. Next to my husband, two women almost came to blows when one muscled in on the other's seating area. I covered my kids' ears on several occasions to prevent them learning a colorful selection of curse words. And if you want to see the world record for tattooed grandmas, I'd suggest the Spicewood Derby.

But perhaps the most surprising discovery was how much I enjoyed it. I never expected cars throttling each other to be my thing. But once it started, I was hooked. And not just me. When an air horn sounded to call a halt to the first round, my girls and I stood and stamped the bleachers with the rest of the crowd. "More!" we all shouted at the top of our lungs.

And more we received. Cars caught fire! The "shark" car was hit so hard its decorative eyeball popped out! By the grand finale, cars and their broken pieces, not to mention the shark "eyeball," lay scattered in the arena dirt. The final two cars each went at each other with bare-knuckled deliberateness, attempting to inflict irreparable damage.

I liked it. I really, *really* liked it. Waiting for the next round of destruction kept us on the edge of our seats. Who knew what would happen? Fires, flips, dramatic crunches? *Bring. It. On!*

I bet the prophet Jonah would have loved a good demolition derby. Hang with me and I'll explain . . . Many of us are familiar with the first half of Jonah's story: God asks him to go to Nineveh to preach; Jonah heads in the opposite direction. Caught in a storm at sea, Jonah is cast overboard and swallowed by a fish. When Jonah repents, the fish throws him up and God gives him another chance.

Nineveh, where God wanted Jonah to preach, was the capital of Assyria, the country brutally devouring the world. The Assyrians attacked the Northern Kingdom of Israel and defeated it. They were merciless, vicious, cruel. They achieved victory and so totally erased the memory of those they conquered that the ten tribes who once lived in the Northern Kingdom of Israel are now considered "lost."

God asks Jonah to go to Nineveh to preach that the jig is up. The demolition derby is about to begin and God's driving the Chrysler Imperial!

What a terrifying assignment! Imagine what the vicious, pagan people in Nineveh will do to some foreigner with the gall to challenge their public policy! We might imagine that Jonah ran because he was afraid of delivering God's message to such bloodthirsty people. But that's not it at all. Jonah didn't flee out of fear. He ran because he didn't want the people in Nineveh to have a chance to change. Jonah, like most people in Judah, longed to see God zero in on Assyria and put the pedal to the metal. If Nineveh is going down in flames, Jonah doesn't want to be the air horn that grinds it to a halt. So he runs.

But after the fish incident, Jonah realizes he doesn't have much choice. Our reluctant prophet goes to Nineveh, but his heart still isn't in it. Prophets who care repeat their message, give examples, share object lessons, tell stories. They preach for years. Their prophecies fill books. Jonah gives the people of Nineveh just *one sentence* (Jonah 3:4).

But here's the crazy thing: this half-hearted prophecy shakes Nineveh to its core. The king takes off his finery and puts on a burlap sack. He asks his people to do the same. They go into mourning, stop eating, even make their animals participate. The people of Nineveh beg God to turn off the Imperial's engine and spare them. And God does! Hurray! Right? Thousands of sinners have repented. An entire nation has had a change of heart. Everyone should be happy, right? Jonah has to be the happiest prophet in history.

Nope. Jonah is beside himself. He, in effect, throws the keys to the Imperial back at God, demanding God restart the engines of destruction. Nineveh is owed a brutal comeuppance. The demolition derby can't stop now!

If you're like me, you tend to think of sin as a choice, an action, something you *do*. In this case, the sin was doing nothing. First, Jonah tried to avoid God's call. Then, he did the very least. He acted obedient, but his heart wasn't in it. Jonah would have happily cheered from the sidelines as Nineveh got its comeuppance.

When would you rather say nothing, do nothing, or go the opposite direction than help someone you dislike receive God's mercy? Are there people you would like to see suffer? Maybe corrupt CEOs who saved their own fortunes as they flushed their workers' pensions down the drains? What about the murderer on death row? Or that politician you vehemently disagree with?

Imagine if God asked you to speak to such a person so he or she might avert destruction. Don't we all understand why Jonah wanted to look the other way and allow God's vengeance to play out?

The book of Jonah begins with Jonah fleeing to the ocean and ends with him fleeing to the desert. In the desert, Jonah takes shelter under a dying plant, watching Nineveh from a distance, hoping the demolition derby will begin. God approaches to ask a question: "Really? Is this really where your heart is, Jonah? Bent on destruction, unable to accept mercy?"

A breath . . .

And the story ends. Right there, with a question and no answer. We never learn what Jonah said.

Stories without endings invite us deep inside them. What happened? Did Jonah die in the desert, or relent? Did he change his heart, or remain bitter? Stories like this invite us to supply the ending, to fill it in with the choices we make.

We have all found ourselves in places like Jonah's. We've all regretted God's mercy, or found others undeserving of it.

All around us is a real-life demolition derby. God is calling you out of the stands where you have been sitting, watching, and maybe even cheering, and into the fray. You can be the one to stop the destruction. Your voice, your words. They don't have to be eloquent; you just have to have the courage and hope to speak them.

Try This

- Put a lime or lemon down the disposal in your sink and watch it get cut to ribbons. Is there a person, a group of people, or a political party you would like to see get their day of reckoning? How would it be for God to ask you to help that person or group avoid disaster? Hold a whole lemon or lime and pray for that group or person—that they would know God's love; that they would have the chance to change; that they would take that opportunity.

- Most of us have at least one person we need to forgive. Who is that? Write, call, or visit that person to offer them your forgiveness. Or perhaps you need to ask someone to forgive you? Take time to do that this week.

21

Adrift in the Storm

Meeting God in Devil's Cove

I have told you all this so that you may have peace in me. Here on earth you will have many trials and sorrows. But take heart, because I have overcome the world.

JOHN 16:33

I NEVER GAVE ANCHORS much thought. Not until the storm in Devil's Cove . . . but I'm getting ahead of myself.

My church challenged me to find God at Hippie Hollow, a (no lie) nudist beach outside of Austin on Lake Travis. I wasn't sure if they were joking, and even though there is no place that God avoids, there are things I'd rather not do. So, I turned my attention to the other infamous lake spot—Devil's Cove. Locals told me that on certain holidays there are so many boats lashed together inside the cove that you could step from one to the other without ever getting wet. It's one giant, floating rave. I would look for God there. Bonus: I could keep my clothes on.

A couple of friends and I borrowed a boat and I brought my binoculars. You know, so I could find God at a safe distance. It didn't work. I quickly learned you can't see inside Devil's Cove from the lake (which explains its appeal among the party crowd). Lots of bad things can happen when nobody can see you. To find God, we had to commit. We drove the boat between the cliffs lining the entrance and into Devil's Cove.

It reminded me of when the rebels in Star Wars approach the Death Star. Everyone gave our driver, Scott, advice, which ended up sounding like what Han told Chewy: "Keep your distance. But don't *look* like you're keeping your distance. I don't know! Fly casual."

We didn't belong. True party people would know it immediately. Yes, I was with a great group of Austin friends, but we all have kids, some of whom are teens. We're too old to be cool anymore. We worried we'd be laughed right out of the place.

As we rounded the corner, braced for the worst, we saw . . . a rather bland scene. Lots of boats, including a houseboat and two colossal yachts. But they held normal people. A few jet skis darted in and out, but not dangerously. There was music, but I knew the words to some of the songs. People floated and chatted, put on sunscreen, and handed out pool noodles. Some were drinking, but none were wild. It was . . . tame.

It shames me to admit it, but we became the real standouts of Devil's Cove that day. Not because of our behavior, but because of our inability to set an anchor. Well, *my* inability to set an anchor.

I don't know why I offered to help. Probably because nobody else stepped up. Someone needed to help, to figure it out, and I thought, how hard could this be? It's an anchor! You drop it in, it sinks to the bottom, and presto: it will hold the boat in place. I dropped the anchor into the lake, let it sink, felt at ease. I was done. In my defense, others on the boat agreed with me. My friend Scott was the lone dissenter. "I don't think that caught," he warned.

"Look at how taut the line is," I said, giving the rope a gentle tug. "It's down there." Scott tried to clarify his concern, asking if the anchor was "set." I didn't know what that word meant, but I felt like we were "all set" to go. So I said, "Yes!"

I have no idea why my friends trusted me. Maybe because I said it with such confidence? Maybe because I'm their pastor and they felt like they had to agree with my terrible logic? Maybe because this was a borrowed boat, and none of us actually knew what we were doing? Whatever it was, I had declared the anchor "set," so everyone jumped in the lake.

But Scott was right. The anchor needs to be more than "down there." It must be firmly attached to an unmoving rock. Which it most definitely was *not*. Our boat began to drift away, backwards, toward the rocky shore. "Oh, no!" everyone said. Feeling responsible, I grabbed one of the ropes hanging off the side of the boat and attempted to kick and swim the boat away from the shore (you can imagine how effective that was). People on other boats started to stare. Scott jumped back on and started the boat in the nick of time, idling it away from the rocks.

We tried again. This time, the guys set the anchor. Now that men were in charge, it was sure to be fine, right? We began to enjoy the cove again. A friend swam up to me and asked if I'd seen God yet. Maybe those ducklings in the middle of Devil's Cove? The joy of good friends? Teamwork?

"I keep thinking it's the anchor," I admitted. But I couldn't complete my thought because the boat slipped away again and my friend and my husband frantically swam to catch it, start the motor, and back it away from the rocky shoreline yet again.

This time, the guys anchored the boat to the shore. Finally! If we can see it, it will be fine. Right?

Sort of. It was sort of fine. Until the storm hit.

Summer thunderstorms can sneak up on you, especially on that side of the lake, with its high cliffs. Devil's Cove is nestled within tall canyon walls. We didn't see the dark clouds until they were almost overhead. Even then, we only noticed when a colossal gust of wind hit. In its wake, the temperature dropped 10 degrees in a matter of seconds and the heavy smell of ozone filled our nostrils. We looked up to see dark clouds cresting the cliff walls. Oh, no!

It got worse. When the wind hit, it pulled the boat free, yet again, from its "anchor." Only this time, the wind was not a gentle breeze, but storm-level gusts. It drove our boat, not toward the shore, but out toward the other crafts anchored in the center of the cove! Once again, Scott made it back to the boat and shouted from the captain's seat toward the slower swimmers still in the lake. "I have to start this—get over here *now*!" I was the only one who made it.

We avoided a crash with the other vessels but heard something just as bad. All around us, motors roared to life, anchors were pulled up, and revelers began to gun it for the narrow entrance to the cove. Rain began to fall in huge, fat drops. A grey sheet of heavier rain loomed, minutes away.

Scott and I looked back in horror to where the rest of our friends bobbed in the water. They were stuck in between the entrance to Devil's Cove and a semi-drunken fleet of boats trying to get out. Our friends were floating in the middle of a mass exodus. And the rain was making it harder and harder to see them.

"Stick your arms up!" I yelled as the first of the other boats roared past. I was about to cry; I was so afraid they would be killed before we could reach them.

Scott was amazing—steering the boat through the wind and rain to reach our friends. The water had become choppy and rough. I knelt at the back, ready to pull out my friends, my husband. Thunder rumbled. The water pitched the boat up and down and once again, we were in danger of being pushed into the shore. "Hurry!" Scott yelled, "I have to start the motor soon or we'll crash."

I'd gotten only two people on board.

Does faith ever feel that way? Like it's easier on days when the sun is shining and everything is going right?

What happens when the bottom drops out?

When you lose your job?

When a contract falls through?

When she leaves you?

Suddenly a storm you didn't see coming blows you away from safety and toward a rocky crash. You look around for something strong to grab onto, any place, but all you see is the moving water, the lashing wind, the sheets of rain.

Jesus warns us: This world will contain trouble, storms. But when the world turns liquid, there is always one solid thing we can grab onto: "Take heart, because I have overcome the world" (John 16:33). On pleasant days, it's important to have a good anchor (and know how to use it). It keeps you from looking like an idiot or getting into a scrape. But you *desperately* need an anchor when winds howl and the waters churn.

A pastor named John discovered this truth firsthand. John was devoted and pious: he got up every day at 5 a.m. to pray, he fasted twice a week, he considered going to get a haircut important because it supported his barber. But though John looked pious on the outside, inside he had no anchor. He was going through the motions but didn't have the assurance that he was even one of God's children. Eventually, Pastor John decided to be a missionary—the ultimate sacrifice. Maybe this would help his faith! John could reach the isolated mission field only by boat. He wrote his friend, "My chief motive is the hope of saving my own soul."

On the journey, a ferocious storm struck. The boat began to flounder, and it appeared all on board would die, swept away and drowned. Pastor John was terrified, along with almost everyone else. John had nothing solid to hold onto as he faced death. But a few passengers on the boat responded differently. They held each other's hands and sang hymns with steady voices. Pastor John longed for such a strong anchor.

When he returned from his missionary journey—which was, as you might suspect, a failure—someone invited Pastor John to a Bible study. He really didn't have the heart for it, but he went. And as John sat there, his heart became anchored. He realized it wasn't what he did for God that secured his place in eternity, it was God's grace *to him.*

John felt accepted, loved, and secure, for the first time in his life. He became a new person—still rigorous, but no longer attempting to earn salvation. He knew the peace of those who sang in the storm. Pastor John Wesley, founder of the Methodist Church, found an anchor for his soul. When he faced death again, this time as an old man, he used his last feeble breath to say, "Best of all, God is with us!"

That day on the lake, the wind and rocks forced us to leave our remaining friends behind a second time and circle back around. The rain lashed and the boat heaved. As I watched my husband bobbing in the water, I lambasted myself for not knowing how to anchor the boat. The anchor was good, strong, and ready. I just hadn't taken time to learn how to use it. And now, three lives were in danger.

On the next attempt, we were able to haul everyone into the boat. We then made our miserable way home through the chilly, lashing rain. As soon as I entered my house, I grabbed a towel and sat down with my laptop. I googled how to set an anchor, watching several experts demonstrate the proper technique. My boat anchoring skills are improving, but the anchor in my heart was set long ago.

God's anchor holds. Always.

There is nothing you can face—no darkness, doubt, pain, sin, betrayal, or loss—that can break God's anchor. You are loved. You are chosen. God will bring you through the storm. God is a constant refuge in a world that's pitching about. The work has been done. Just let the great captain set this anchor in your heart. It will hold.

Try This

- Sit by a marina, dock, or place where boats anchor. Or find running water and look at the trees along the riverbank. The writer of Hebrews calls God's promises an anchor for his soul (6:19). As you look out at those "anchored" things, what speaks to you? If you were to put into words God's work in your life, what metaphor would you choose?

- A woman in my church who was dying of cancer described a special place in prayer where she met Jesus. Whenever she was afraid, discouraged, or drained, she imagined herself in this place, with the Lord. Do you have a place, in your heart or this world, where you delight to meet with Jesus? If not, why not create one? Think of a place, real or imagined, where you would delight to be. Fill in the details. Sunny or cloudy? What are the colors, smells, textures? What does it feel like to be there? When you feel adrift, ask Jesus to meet with you there in prayer. Ask Jesus to anchor you.

22

(Don't) Give Up

Graffiti and Voodoo Donuts

In the same way, let your good deeds shine out for all to see, so that everyone will praise your heavenly Father.

MATTHEW 5:16

"Jeremiah the Innocent" is one of Austin's most iconic pieces of street art. He's a smiling frog-alien, painted in black on a brick wall at the corner of Twenty-First and Guadalupe, across from the University of Texas (UT) campus. Jeremiah has greeted decades of students and visitors with his happy "Hi, how are you?" slogan.

Students at UT asked me to help them look for God on campus, so I joined Sarah, a recent graduate, on a morning walk. Seeing Jeremiah, we paused long enough to take the requisite photo.

As I started to leave, my eyes caught a message scrawled in black on the sidewalk at Jeremiah's feet: "Don't Give Up." I pointed it out to Sarah, thinking this just might be the shortest search for God in history. But Sarah didn't share my excitement. I could almost see her body curl in, protective, distressed.

"Pastor Laura . . . that . . . " Sarah struggled to put what she was feeling into words. Then she sighed, "That was terrible."

"*What* was terrible?" I looked again at the hopeful message, completely baffled.

"Let's walk away from here," Sarah suggested. As we put distance between us and the painted words, Sarah began to explain. One day a few years ago, students awoke to find posters and graffiti everywhere across campus. Each bore the same message: "Give up." Often, the words were accompanied by the outline of a razor blade. The vicious message had been pasted to telephone poles, written on sidewalks, graffitied over stop signs. The vandals had even gone to Jeremiah the Innocent to paint the dark message on the sidewalk at his feet.

"So what happened next?" I asked. You see, the message I'd read wasn't the one the vandal had scrawled. It had been transformed, from hateful and violent to loving and hopeful. All with the addition of one word: Don't. *Don't* give up.

"Well," Sarah said, "that's the good part." A few nights later, somebody went through campus and changed every single one of the graffiti messages. To this day, nobody knows who. As I walked, I tried to picture that person. Like everyone else, they awoke to find their community marred by evil. Those hateful words, "Give up," assaulted them over and over as they made their way to morning classes, to lunch, to evening labs. This person likely overheard expressions of shock, sorrow, outrage. Maybe they thought or prayed about what could be done.

And then, whoever they were, they went to the hardware store, and got a can of paint. That unknown person found every sentence on campus and amended the message over, and over, and over:

Don't give up.

Don't give up.

Don't give up.

Whoever it was that revised the message, they changed the story for all who encountered it thereafter. When I saw the updated message, there was only kindness and hope. The evil intent had been transformed.

Being people of faith means God gives us the power to change the story, no matter how dark it's gotten. We, God's people, must do more than lament what the world is coming to; we must actively resist. We must take loving action that lets God's light shine. No matter how bad it's gotten, the light will always win. But we must get out there. Saint Francis said, "It is no use walking anywhere to preach unless our walking is our preaching."

Our preaching, our witness, happens *on the journey*, or not at all. We show our faith in how we live. As Jesus says, we are to let our light shine. We do that when others see our "good deeds" and praise God (Matt 5:16). People glimpse God in our good actions. Not our good thoughts. Not our good beliefs. People see God in what we do, in how we live, in what we say, our good works. When you wake up to find the world has gotten darker, don't close the door and try to put it out of your mind! Get out there and shine the light of God's love.

I seriously doubt the person who changed the message had vast experience with vandalism, spray paint, or graffiti. And yet they stepped way beyond their comfort zone to bring light to the darkness. One bad person can do harm, but one good person can change the story.

In ways great and small, we fight back against the darkness. We fight the darkness with light.

Later that evening, I saw how beautiful good actions could be. I was on Sixth Street with four college students, searching for God in a place most people only look for a good time.

After making a loop of the bar scene, we finished up at Voodoo Donuts. Voodoo offers mega-bargains in the wee hours of the morning. We discovered five-gallon *buckets* of donuts for ten dollars!

In our kitchen is a little sign that says, "Yeah, abs are great . . . but have you tried donuts?" So I am not unfamiliar with donuts and the quantities in which they are sold. But a construction bucket of donuts was a whole new level of delight, especially at that price. I paid (big spender!) and we settled in. It was a hot summer night and, for some reason, Voodoo eschews air conditioning, so even at midnight, we were sweating.

While we were eating and talking about where we had noticed God on Sixth Street, a man in a wheelchair rolled in. We said hello and when he came back, asking for money, we offered to share our donuts. "No," he said. "What would really help is three dollars." Some of the students told him they didn't have money, which as far as I know, was true.

The man got belligerent in a snap. "If you don't want to help me, don't lie. Just say it to my face, 'I don't want to help *you*!'" I was taken aback. The anger, the hatred, was like a slap in the face when only kindness had been offered. Before I could respond, before I could even think of how to respond, one of the students who had been silent until that point stood up.

His name was Ryan and he rose so he could reach his wallet, pulling it from his back pocket and opening it up. Inside was one twenty-dollar bill. That's it. Ryan pulled that twenty out and gave it to the belligerent man. All the money he had.

The man grabbed the money and rolled away. Not a word of thanks. Not a word of acknowledgement. We sat in stunned silence. After a few moments, one of the students asked the question on all our minds . . . why had Ryan done it?

Ryan looked down at his hands, holding his empty wallet, and said, "Every day, as I walk across campus, or to my car, or to the student center, someone asks me for help. *Every day.* Often twice. I never have cash, so I can't help. I promised myself next time I had cash, I would help anyone who asked me."

Ryan was the student who quietly begged me not to spend my last ten dollars buying everyone's donuts. Ryan drove a ridiculously beat-up car and his sneakers were quite worn. But he had promised himself that when he had cash and someone needed help, he would offer it. Ryan found a way to bring light to the darkness.

When asked about how he knew it would be used well, Ryan shrugged. "I'm not as worried about that. I did what God put on my heart. I will have enough tomorrow. And perhaps it will make a big difference for him."

Each of us has the power to change the message. To change hate and hopelessness into love and encouragement. To give to those who ask without judging if they are worthy.

Mother Teresa said, "There are no great acts. Only small acts, done with great love." We help others find God in our community when we choose to do good in the face of evil. Small acts of good force the darkness back.

Try This

- The children at my church create "Random Acts of Kindness" (RAK) bags. They write a note or draw a picture and put it in a gallon Ziploc bag. Then they add a juice box, peanut butter crackers, energy bar, and some gummies. The kids hand these out to people in the church so we can carry them in our cars. When we see someone who is hungry and begging, we can meet their eyes, smile, and help. Make a set of RAK bags and hand them out. Or get some dollar bills and do as Ryan did—offer them whenever someone asks. What are those interactions like?

- What small acts of goodness could you plan and prepare for? My friend Jon carries change when he crosses the bridge into and out of Mexico, to put into the hands of little children who reach through the international bridge's slats for help. Another woman knits Hello Kitty dolls for kids who don't have birthday presents. Teams of believers cook meals throughout the week at different churches to take to the homeless. What action could you take?

23

Ladies' Night

God amongst Cage Dancers

For this is how God loved the world: He gave his one and only Son, so that everyone who believes in him will not perish but have eternal life.

JOHN 3:16

MIDNIGHT ON A CRISP Friday night found me loitering around the door of a nightclub, waiting for the five young Air Force officers who had suggested this locale as a place to look for God. I glanced down at my tight black pants—too much? I had two little girls sleeping at home and though I was just twenty-nine, I was dangerously out of my element. Taking a deep breath, I reminded myself once more that no one here would recognize me. And if they did, well, what happens in Vegas . . .

Every time the bouncer opened the doors to admit more patrons, music and smoke poured over me. After what felt like an awkward eternity, I finally spotted my friends and happily joined the group, feeling protected by their familiarity. As they led me inside, the guy at the door smiled. "Nice pants," he said.

"Let's start with the lay of the land," a young lieutenant suggested. She veered left and led us toward a room that played Tejano with lots of line dancing and bright, flashing lights. In the center of the room people bunched up in tight concentric circles, moving like a single organism. None of my guides felt a pull to that room, so we moved on.

In the center of the next room was a wooden dance floor strewn with sawdust. Patrons in jeans and boots were partnered up, spinning and two-stepping. I desperately wanted to linger in the safe cocoon of that room, with its familiar music and dance steps I knew. I could lean up against the wooden railing and if anyone asked me to dance, I'd know the steps: from two-step, to jitterbug, to waltz. I even know a few line dances, though it pains me to admit it.

But I hadn't come to find God in the safety of the familiar. I had come to meet God in the unknown. So I turned away from the country-western room. The last two venues were the most challenging. In one, female bartenders in short skirts danced in high heels on top of the bar. Below them, patrons gaped unabashedly up. Occasionally, a bartender reached down to pull someone up to grind with her on the bar top. The loudest cheers and wolf whistles came when she chose a woman.

But even that felt tame in comparison to the main room, which we came to last. The largest space, this room was also the darkest and most crowded, filled with smoke, strobes, and high-tempo club music. High above the floor hung metal cages, accessed by narrow steps. I watched clubgoers climb up to dance in the cages, their bodies grinding against the metal bars and against each other. Instead of walking around the edge of this room, my friends went right through it, winding us slowly across the floor, beneath the gyrating cage dancers, and through the heat of a hundred bodies. As we made our slow progress, I had one thought: "Please God, don't let someone pull me up into a cage."

My heart pounded as I made my way to the edge of the room and an empty seat. It was my one goal—that seat—and the small bit of safety it offered. But no sooner had I sat down than a woman leaned over to yell at me above the music. The chair was hers. I had to leave. Red-faced, I got up and walked over to the wall, leaned against it, and considered the scene before me. The sooner I found God, the sooner I could go home. Oh, home . . . with my husband and my kids, all asleep like I should be. Oh, home . . . my little house under the oak trees, so peaceful. And so far away from this loud, confusing place.

Smoke filled my nostrils and sank into my clothes. Searchlights swung around the room, illuminating all those bodies, circling around and around, just like my mind as I searched for God. I longed to turn away, to close my eyes, to leave. I could not see any evidence of God—only drinking,

lust, and self-abandon. "Where are you?" I whispered, the prayer lost in the riot of noise.

American nightclubs did not invent vice. It's been around since that first sweet, tart bite of forbidden fruit. Vice grinds away in the places church-goers avoid. But let's be honest. Though most church folks don't go in for the obvious "dancing in cages" type vice, *everyone* is tempted to slip into the darkness at some point.

The book of Judges records how Israel succumbed, again and again, to the dark allure of temptation. In one account, a man is traveling when he's attacked by the people in the town where he's chosen to spend the night. To save himself, the man shoves the woman he's traveling with into the arms of the mob. He escapes, but they gang-rape her until she is almost unconscious and leave her dying. She uses her last strength to crawl back to the door he's locked himself behind, collapsing on the threshold. In the morning he finds her, dead. He carries her body home, only to cut it into pieces and mail one piece to each of the twelve tribes (who each lived in a different section of Israel) with a note explaining what happened. The country reacts as we'd expect. "Everyone who saw it said, 'Such a horrible crime has not been committed in all the time since Israel left Egypt. Think about it! What are we going to do? Who's going to speak up?'" (Judg 19:30).

"*Who* will do something about this?" The book of Judges is about generations of people asking that question. Prophets arise; people repent. Prophets die; people regress. There are periods of redemption, but then the darkness swallows it all up once more. The pattern we see in Judges is repeated, in some form, throughout the Old Testament.

But finally, dawn breaks on an entirely new day. Jesus steps into the middle of humanity's grime and filth. God comes into the very world that makes us want to hide our faces. Jesus doesn't stand at a safe distance and beckon the lost and broken to his side. He doesn't insist people get them-selves cleaned up before they approach him. Jesus goes to places where sin is the worst and speaks with the people there, not to berate them, but to give them a chance to come home.

Have you heard of John 3:16? It says, "For this is how God loved the world: He gave his one and only Son, so that everyone who believes in him will not perish but have eternal life." But have you ever read it in light of

Judg 19? Have you ever considered the *power* of God's coming into the filthy fray? God sees our perverse behavior and vice. But God doesn't retreat to heaven and put us out of mind. God comes closer. God loves us despite our sickness. God comes to live in this fallen world to save us.

"Where are you, God?" I prayed when I wanted to hide my face. And suddenly I knew. God was *with me*. God is with us when we remember that the people grinding away in the corners, the people who won't share their chair, the people dancing on the bar, are God's beloved children. This nightclub is exactly the type of place Jesus would visit, and these are the very people Jesus would speak to with love.

Believers like me often keep themselves in clean, tidy places. But those aren't the places Jesus chooses. Jesus would be right in the middle of the bar scene. He is accused of being a drunkard, morally compromised, even called an agent of Satan. But Jesus continues going into the darkness because that's where the people who need him are.

For God so loved . . .
the bartender grinding on the bar
the men gawking,
the women in cages,
the people in the smoke,
that God sent us Jesus.

Still today, God sends us into the fray. As we answer that call, we learn to see every person as a child God loves deeply. We follow Jesus by being present in people's lives within and beyond the club. We follow Jesus when we step into the darkness so God's light can shine there.

Try This

- Where are the places "good Christians" in your community don't go? This week, could you visit, just once? Take a friend for support or find a "native" who is comfortable there and ask them to show you around. Ask God to show you where the Spirit is already moving in that place, among those folks.

- What are the struggles in your community? If you don't know, check in with a school counselor, community health worker, or even local police and fire departments. The people in Judges ask, "Who is going to speak up?" Ponder who you rely on to help with such needs (local government, aid organizations, your church or pastor). What might you, your family, your friend group, your business, or your neighborhood do about pain in your community?

24

Trail of Crumbs

God on "Dirty Sixth"

Jesus entered Jericho and made his way through the town. There was a man there named Zacchaeus. He was the chief tax collector in the region, and he had become very rich.

LUKE 19:1–2

A SUMMER NIGHT: hot, humid, approaching midnight. College students were leading me from the lonely parking garage where we'd parked and they'd climbed, clown-car-style, out of my SUV. Our goal: a concert on Sixth Street. Sixth Street is Austin's bar and nightclub scene, sometimes called "Dirty Sixth" because of the sleezy vibe. Thus, a perfect place to look for God!

As we waited for the walk signal on one bustling corner, a homeless man crossed from the opposite direction, carrying a take-out container with a few scraps of food. Passing us, he stuck his fingers into the container and dropped a morsel on the ground near my feet. Tuna, maybe? Or noodles? I didn't lean down to make sure of the contents. In fact, I didn't think much about it at all except to be glad it hadn't fallen on my foot.

But as we waited at the light, Cooper, one of the students, spoke up: "Look! Do you think he was leaving a trail?" Cooper pointed from the morsel at my feet to a line of white food scraps that extended away into the night.

128

Of all we saw that night, God spoke to me most powerfully right there at the beginning, through a homeless man. And his fragile trail of crumbs.

I know nearly nothing about that homeless man. But his trail of crumbs told me that there was a place he wanted to be able to find again. Maybe that trail was meant to lead him back to the spot he called home. Or to food. Or to a location where he asked for money. Whatever the place, the man wanted to be able to return, to find his way back.

But I suspect this man also knew his own limitations. Perhaps he knew he didn't remember well. Maybe he'd been lost in the past. He might have known he needed help. So he left himself a map. A fragile little trail he hoped to follow back to someplace good. This man did not want to be lost.

None of us *want* to be lost physically, emotionally, or spiritually. And yet, so often the way isn't obvious. Lost can happen in lots of ways.

What do I do now that I'm retired?

How am I supposed to raise these teens?

How does faith become part of the fabric of my life?

Is there anything beyond this grief?

I'm reminded of another man who felt lost. Nobody around him noticed, and if they had, they wouldn't have cared. Because the lost man was a tax collector. Every year, this tax collector paid Rome the taxes assessed for his entire region . . . in advance! Then Rome let him and his employees collect the payments. Anything above what Rome required was profit.

He was rich.

He was powerful.

He was . . . lost.

The tax collector knew he was lost. He felt it with growing sorrow each day as he went out to oversee the collection of taxes. He didn't want this life anymore, but he had no idea how to change. No idea how to find his way home. Or if anybody even wanted him back after all his sins.

Tax collectors defiled things, so this man wasn't allowed into God's temple in Jerusalem. No good person would even allow him into their home. He was *unclean*. People hated him for colluding with Rome, for robbing his own people to line his pockets. But in the eyes of the faithful, his job was more than loathsome. It was unclean. It tainted his soul. And if they invited him over, he'd make them, their home, their kids, unclean, just by being there. Only other tax collectors would visit his home, invite him over, or share a meal, a small community of the damned.

Then one day, the tax collector hears that Jesus is coming through town. Jesus—the Messiah—God's Savior. Jesus, whom the demons obey. Jesus, who heals the sick. Jesus, whose inner circle includes . . . a former tax collector! Oh, this man longs to get a glimpse of Jesus, to see his face. Maybe just a look at Jesus will help him find his way.

But that's what everyone else in town wants: a glimpse. And they are all taller. For once, the ordinary people could stick it to the tax collector. Nobody moves over to make room for him. Every time he tries to find a hole to slip through, a way to see, somebody blocks him. I can imagine them delighting in keeping this dirty, sinful man away from the Messiah. They don't know his pain. They don't know he is longing to change. They only know he has hurt them.

But the tax collector doesn't give up. He runs ahead and climbs a tree. In this time, grown men didn't run; it was considered humiliating. And they certainly didn't climb trees. I imagine the town elbowing each other as the tax collector makes a spectacle of himself.

But when Jesus walks past the tree, sees the town laughing, and looks up, he doesn't join in the mockery. Jesus doesn't yell or scold. Jesus calls the man's name: "Zacchaeus! Quick, come down! I must be a guest in your home today" (Luke 19:5).

This was beyond belief, beyond hope! Zacchaeus had hoped to *see* Jesus, just a glimpse, just something to help him find his way. Now, the person everyone wanted to see is going to *stay* with him. Jesus has chosen Zacchaeus' house. Such an honor!

For the first time in ages, Zacchaeus isn't lost. He runs straight home, setting things in order with purpose and clarity. As he welcomes Jesus, the next steps became clear too: Half of all he has, and that is quite a lot, will be sold and given to the poor. And if he has stolen anything, he'll pay it back fourfold. Zacchaeus is sorry. He will make amends for his sins. He will help those who have the least. Zacchaeus repents.

But the town doesn't lift him up on their shoulders, rejoicing. They cross their arms tight across their chests, grumbling. This sinful tax collector has made his bed and now he should have to lie in it, filthy mess that it is! The town grumbles about Jesus, too, suggesting that if Jesus really is the Savior, he should spend his time with more deserving people.

But Jesus' response is different:

"Salvation has come to this home today . . . for the Son of Man came to seek and save those who are lost" (Luke 19:9–10). Many scholars contend that the entire gospel of Luke is summarized right there: Jesus comes to seek and save the lost.

A man on Sixth Street, trying to find the way back.

A man in a tree, trying to find the way home.

And all of us, just trying to find our way.

I've got good news! The lost are the heart of Jesus' mission. Jesus comes to find the lost. Jesus comes to save the lost.

Lost is not shameful.

Lost is not permanent.

Lost is not the end.

Jesus is looking for you. Right now. When you start to look for God, when you find a tree and scramble up, when you open your Bible, when you start to pray, you'll find Jesus looking right back, calling your name. Ready to spend time with you. You don't have to be lost anymore.

This is no trail of bread crumbs. It's the joyful thunderbolt that says life, from this day on, can be different. *Will* be different.

We are all, in one way or another, tree climbers—used to seeking, striving, earning every little scrap we get. Used to paying the price for our sins. And paying. And paying. And then Jesus comes. *Come down, I'm here. I'm with you*, he says. All our seeking—our trying to reach the divine on our own—is silenced when we learn that the divine is reaching out for us.

Here we were trying to find the way home. But home came to get us. To seek us. And to save us.

Try This

- Get yourself lost somewhere in town—a place that is unfamiliar to you but still safe. You might have a friend drive you, blindfolded, to an unknown space and leave you. Notice what you feel. Attempt to find your way back (make sure you have your phone so you can get a map or call that friend, if needed). What do you use to guide you? How does this experience call up times you've felt spiritually or emotionally lost?

- Is there someone whose faith you admire? Grab a coffee with that person and ask them their story. Did they have an experience of being lost, then found? What did lost feel like? How did God call them home? What helped?

25

Cuffed to a Bench

Finding God in Jail

But now you are free from the power of sin.

ROMANS 6:22A

"My mom has been to jail!"

The fifth-grade Sunday school class was discussing Paul's prison letters. My daughter, making the connection, chimed in with this little chestnut.

I can only imagine the horrified silence. The teachers' eyes cutting quickly toward each other in a silent conversation about what to say next. *Pastor Laura . . . in jail!?* Nobody ever told them that. But Anna insists . . . my mom was arrested! My mom has been handcuffed! My mom has been in jail!

I haven't. Not really. Nothing close to the pain, isolation, and suffering being in prison entails. Our society is grappling right now with big questions about crime, punishment, race, and justice. These are important conversations, and important for people of faith. My experience is so much less than the reality of jail that I didn't know how much it would have to offer. But someone asked me to look for God in jail. And this was as close as I could get. Even though it was a shadow of the real thing, I have never forgotten that experience. I met God in a powerful way. As we continue to seek a society that is just for all, I hope this little window helps you and spurs greater thinking about the larger issues involved.

I have this conviction that there is nowhere on earth we won't encounter God, even the darkest corners. Each year I discover God in some new, challenging location. One day, someone asked me to get arrested and look for God. I think he said it as a joke, but the idea just wouldn't leave me alone. So I called the chief of police in the small town down the road from my church. He was a member of my congregation. Not surprisingly, Rusty wasn't too keen on arresting me, even fake-arresting me. Then I shared why I wanted to do it. I wanted to have the experience, as real as possible, and look for God.

Rusty had to check it out with supervisors but finally everyone agreed. I was happy: I could look for God somewhere I'd never been able to before. But as I got into my car to drive to the neighboring town and its police station, my hands began to shake on the steering wheel.

I took a deep breath, trying to talk sense to myself. This isn't real, I reminded my hands. But they weren't getting the message. I took another breath. "Not real," I reiterated to my heart as it began to race. My body stubbornly ignored my calm words. I was scared. Really scared. Huh.

You see, on some level, I knew it wouldn't *feel* fake. And it didn't. I went in the front door of the police station. There they told me, if I was still serious, that this wasn't the door I'd be using. I needed to go back outside. An officer would meet me. I walked outside and waited. An officer emerged from an unmarked side door. He met me on the sidewalk and took away my keys and purse. He pulled my arms behind my back and cuffed my hands together.

I stood shackled in plain view of everyone passing through town that day. I had not considered this part. What if someone saw me? The gossip mill in my little town would explode. There is no good way to explain being handcuffed on the police lawn.

I immediately felt the need to get off the street and out of view quickly. I tried to walk away toward the door the officer had used, but he stopped me. I wasn't in control anymore. I was going to stand, cuffed on that lawn, until *he* was ready to walk me inside, by whatever route he chose. It seemed like an eternity passed before he finally put a hand on one of my cuffed arms, and we moved at his pace down the sidewalk and around the back of the building to an entrance I didn't even know was there.

Now two police officers were with me, one on either side. The first one directed me in, unlocked my cuffs, fingerprinted me, then relocked my arms behind me, handcuffing me to a metal bench bolted into the floor. As he did, the other asked basic questions: name, date of birth, height, weight, and address. He opened my purse (without asking) and dug through it to find my wallet. He then opened it and went through that until he located my license, fastening it to the clipboard with the notes.

Then, without a parting word, they left.

I sat alone, handcuffed to a metal bench in the police department.

Physically, I was uncomfortable. There is no way to nonchalantly sit with your hands cuffed behind you. And certainly no way to feel relaxed or even okay. My nose started running. There was no way to wipe it.

I have never felt so alone. No one looked at me. Officers and office workers chatted about weekend plans and schedules. Outside the sun shone and cars passed by on their way to the outdoor shopping mall in our community. Chained to a bench, I was no longer free to join in. I didn't even feel like a real person. True, I could have called out for help at any time. I could have admitted this was too difficult, emotionally and physically, and the officers who arrested me would have immediately unlocked the cuffs. I could have saved face by claiming to have found God, thank you very much for helping me. But I didn't call out. Because if you're actually arrested, that's not one of your options. I stayed put, alone, handcuffed to a bench as the world passed by.

I don't cry a lot, but I wanted to. To ward off that embarrassing situation, I prayed. "Okay, Lord, here I am. I did this to find where you are, so please show me. You said there is no place you won't be. But I am having a hard time."

I sat and I waited. My nose ran. My eyes watered. My arms ached. The free world motored past, unconcerned. And sitting there, I found God. I found God when I realized something so profound, it's been with me ever since that day.

I suddenly understood what sin does to me. It whispers beautiful lies, leading me away from life, and into jail. It promises pleasure and delivers death. We all struggle with sin, whether it's the allure of money, or an addiction, or lust, or one of the hundreds of other things we grapple with throughout our lives. We have all found our hearts in chains. We end up locked to a bench, separated from life.

It's not like I didn't know this. I have read verses about sin. I know the traps it sets and how cunningly they can be disguised as something appealing and wonderful. I would have told you I fully understood it. But now I was living out some horrible prophetic message to myself. *This* is what sin does to us. There is a difference, I discovered, between knowing it in your mind and feeling it. That day, I *felt* it.

And suddenly, a message that had always seemed trite—*Jesus will set you free*—was the one thing I wanted most in this world. I longed to be free. Ached for it.

God met me there in the police station when I understood what it means to say Jesus is the key. Jesus has the power and authority to release me, if only I call out. I must want to leave the sin behind. Just like I could have called out to the officers, all I needed to do to be free from sin was call out to Jesus. But I'd have to want to be free enough to ask for help.

As I sat chained to that bench, understanding the gravity of sin, I asked myself the next question: What has me chained right now? What darkness have I listened to, followed, been chained by? And . . . do I want to be free? Am I ready for a jailbreak? Ready for God to come into the heart of my problems (the things I keep hidden from the world) and bring the key? Yes. Yes, I was.

When I had prayed, asking Jesus to set my heart free from sin, I waited with greater peace. It felt like a very long time. It was likely a few hours before the chief of police came over and asked if I was ready. They unlocked me and I walked out the front door, shaking but changed. I was free of a tangle of sin that has never snared my feet again (although different ones certainly have). Years later, I still look back on that day as a turning point, a day of liberty and release.

What about you? Which sin has you locked up and hog-tied? Today is the day to be set free! This doesn't mean that temptation won't strike again. It will. But God is the great liberator, the breaker of chains, the one who delivers us.

If you are ready to be free, just ask Jesus to help you. Let today be a jailbreak for your soul.

Try This

- Sit outside of a gated community, country club, or other members-only place where you might be able to observe a fence or a barrier, maybe even see the people inside, but not interact with them. Use this "locked-out" space to consider the places sin has you trapped. What life is it robbing you of?

- Find a place where you can be alone and put your hands behind your back, as if cuffed. Sit there until it's uncomfortable. Watch the world pass by. Is there a habit or sin that has you trapped? Jesus can and will set you free. Just ask. Feel your cramped posture release, your hands unbind.

26

God at the Hoity Toit

"You Can't Get from Here to There without a Six-Pack"

*When Jesus heard this, he said, "Healthy people don't need a doctor
—sick people do."*

MATTHEW 9:12

A MAN STANDING IN the parking lot glanced over at us, unzipped his pants, and urinated onto the dusty gravel. I tried not to act as horrified as I felt, but walked around him in a wide circle on my way to the bar's door. I was looking for God at the Hoity Toit bar, and I'd brought a group from my church with me. It certainly wasn't starting well.

Most of the folks I know enjoy a cold beer with their BBQ on Friday nights. Some have a favorite local winery or brewery. But none of us had ever been to the Hoity Toit bar. And the reason was becoming clearer by the second.

I took the lead, taking a deep breath before pushing open the bar's wooden doors, positioned below a sign that proclaims, "The Hoity Toit . . . you can't get from here to there without a six-pack!" Beyond, we found a dimly lit room, lots of neon, and a mix of tables and barstools, all full. Everyone turned to look as we walked in. Seriously—just like we were in one of those Old West saloons in the movies.

The air was filled with smoke and honky-tonk music, but all the conversations trailed off as we walked in. A drunken voice spoke into the awkward silence, "Tourists sit outside." (Get it? With the urinating guy.)

"Oh," I stammered, "we're not tourists . . . we live here. It's just our first time." While tourists in New Braunfels are part of the city's lifeblood, bringing much-needed income to local businesses, they also bring trash, traffic, and resentment. There's a big difference between locals and tourists. Perhaps that's why the patrons were acting so frosty?

Nope. Even learning that we were locals didn't thaw the atmosphere. Nobody replied. Nobody opened their arms to welcome us. Nobody even smiled. They all just turned away, one by one, and resumed their conversations. We stood at the door, unsure, trying to work out our next move. There were no empty seats.

Eventually the bartender jerked a thumb to an open door on the back wall and we threaded past the tables with the regulars into what we discovered was a back room. A *totally empty* back room. I'm not sure if the bartender normally came to your table, or if it was a further sign that we were not encouraged to return to the front section.

For a while, we stayed put, occupying ourselves with the pool table, shuffleboard, and darts that had also been relegated to that space. The regulars remained up front, walking past us only to use the bathroom and casting skeptical looks at us from the corners of their eyes. It might have gone on like that all night.

But my bubbly West Texas-raised friend grabbed my hand and dragged me through the door to the front room. Terri either couldn't read the looks or just knew she could overcome them, because she started in what I assumed was the toughest area: the folks under a neon sign that proclaimed "Asshole Section." Each time Terri moved to a new clump of patrons, I followed in her happy wake, smiling and trying to make conversation.

Things were going really well until someone asked where we worked. Terri and I both worked at the Methodist church in town. Hearing this, an entire section went silent once again, then began to apologize profusely for their foul language.

As the shock wore off, someone bravely asked us the next question, "What are you doing *here?*" I admitted that we had come to the bar to look for God, which I know likely made me sound like I was already three sheets to the wind. A bunch of church people, in a bar, to try to find God? Another patron gave voice to the question on everyone's mind: "Why are you look-ing for *God* in a *bar*?"

I love that question, in all the forms it has taken over the years. And I love getting to share how there is no place in this world where God isn't present. They asked where we had seen evidence of God. And after sharing, I asked them if they had noticed God anywhere. They had. One person had had a terrible week at work. But when she sat down, someone bought her a beer. Another spoke up, at the Hoity Toit, he found support, acceptance, and community with the other self-proclaimed "assholes" under the neon sign. Yet another stuck a thumb at the bartender and said he was an excel-lent listener. And never judged.

God, it turns out, was all over the Hoity Toit bar.

Of course!

Jesus hangs out with "lowlifes" way more than most of us modern-day believers do. In his time on earth, Jesus socialized with drunks, hookers, sell-outs, losers, tax collectors, and Samaritans. Though he never condones sin or sinful lifestyles, Jesus knows broken people need him most. So Jesus spends time in places sinners feel comfortable. Jesus is among them so he can show them the way home to God, the way to a transformed and re-newed life.

But what about us? What about me? What about my church? The folks at the Hoity Toit thought that having a pastor in their bar was weird. It felt weird to me too. I let that roll around in my mind as Terri and I finished making the rounds and returned to the obscurity of the back room. Once there, I commended my friend for her bravery.

"Oh," she said, "I just love people, even the drunk ones."

That's such a Christlike attitude. And one we so often forget. How Jesus loves people, *all* people. And because of that love, our Savior puts himself in places that connect him with people who need him most. He gets a lot of flak for it. People call him names: "glutton," "drunkard," "friend of . . . sinners" (Matt 11:19). I wonder—has my love for the broken ever been strong enough to merit such slander?

The religious folks don't cheer Jesus on. They don't clap when sinners are forgiven, at least not with the same gusto they impart when Jesus heals the sick or feeds the hungry. The religious folks certainly don't join Jesus in visiting dodgy locales to seek out the lost, broken, and stained. Quite frankly, Jesus' behavior appalls them.

After one meal, the Pharisees (some of the holiest folks of the day) pull Jesus' disciples (not Jesus) aside and scold them: "Why does your teacher eat with such scum?" (Matt 9:11).

But Jesus overhears and responds: "Healthy people don't need a doctor—sick people do. . . . I have come to call not those who think they are righteous, but those who know they are sinners" (Matt 9:12–13).

Jesus comes for the broken, the assholes, the people who pee in parking lots. He never holds people, even dirty ones, at arm's length. Jesus gets close. Jesus would never stay in the back room. Jesus knows *being there* matters. Deeply.

Over the next several hours, most of our group made it to the front section of the bar. Eventually, a few folks from the front came to joke with us in the back. I saw the powerful difference "being there" made that night. When it came time to leave, the atmosphere was vastly different than when we'd walked in. Everyone noticed us going and there was almost a collective sigh. "Leaving so soon? Why? Stay a little longer. The night is young."

A table of three I'd been talking to earlier in the night stopped me as I left: two men and a woman. We'd realized that we lived in the same neighborhood earlier that evening. "Come back," one of them said, "be sure to come back and see us. You are welcome here."

I've wondered and wondered about that plea, for that's what it sounded like to me. I've wondered about it for all the years in between then and now. Those folks invited me back to a place I'd resolved to visit just once. Once, I told myself, was better than never.

But is it enough? Shouldn't we push ourselves not just to go, but to return? To return to the places that make us uncomfortable. To return, even to places we wouldn't choose for ourselves, because Jesus calls us to them, and to the people there.

A young woman at our church heard about our visit to the Hoity Toit and sent me a note about a family member who is a regular. She wrote, "He's smart, funny, sincere. He loves his kids and is a very hard worker—but he just cannot get away from the alcohol. . . . He spends most of his money at the Hoity Toit and has lost several homes due to his drinking. All his brothers and sisters had a rough life and all of them have so many things hiding inside. I think his drinking problem must have something to do with this."

This woman closed her letter with these words: "Thanks, Pastor Laura, for not judging these people and for making them feel like someone, even if it was just for a couple of hours."

It *was* just a couple of hours. I wonder if I just vacation in hard areas when Jesus is calling me to be a regular? I wonder if we all fall into that trap. And how we might allow God to lead us into unfamiliar places, uncomfortable places, to sit with the people who are stuck there, not just for a few hours, but long enough to become regulars. Long enough to be God's witnesses there, witnesses to the power of love, healing, and mercy; people who point through the darkness at the doorway that leads to light and life.

Try This

- Visit a hospital or nursing home (places that make most people uncomfortable). Take your church's altar flowers, helium balloons from the dollar store, garden veggies, stickers, or letters from kids. If you have a friendly, well-behaved dog, a nursing home might love for you to bring it along. Or perhaps you play an instrument; could you play in a hallway so patients could hear? Just see if you can go, with whatever skills you have, to connect with lonely or sick people.

- What restaurants, bars, or nightclubs do you drive by regularly? Plan to stop in. Take a couple of friends if you need courage. Go with your eyes open—notice who is there, what type of music is playing, even what people are doing. Be kind; be open to a nudge from God. Conversation with another person would be an amazing starting point.

27

Ciao, Bella

Finding God, Pentecost-Style

Long ago the Lord said to Israel: "I have loved you, my people, with an everlasting love. With unfailing love I have drawn you to myself."

JEREMIAH 31:3

A COUPLE OF YEARS AGO, my family won the lottery . . . at least that's what it felt like. I wrote a grant proposal that was selected by the Lilly Foundation. They gave me and my church funds that provided a time of pastoral sabbatical: three months where I would look for God in foreign countries. Best of all, the whole family, my husband and two girls, were invited to join me.

We allowed ourselves one backpack each and thought carefully about what we most needed for ten weeks of travel. We visited eight countries where seven different languages were spoken. We traveled by plane, then car, ferry, train, and foot.

One of my family's favorite places that summer was Venice. There are lots of reasons it might *not* have been a favorite. It was ridiculously hot and there were throngs of tourists. But when we left the tourist streets, the crowds thinned and ancient Venice opened before us. We wandered with great abandon. It was an island; how lost could we get?

One more thing made Venice a delight—the people. By the time our family took a ferry across the lagoon to Venice, we'd been traveling for a month. Our adventure began in England and Scotland, where we could speak the language and go to church on Sundays. We'd been able to connect with anyone we met, from the store clerks to the people in flats next to us. Going to church on Sundays helped us feel more like we belonged, even far from home. After worship, families had invited us over to their homes for tea, to see their prized Highland cattle, or to visit a church bell tower and learn how the bells were rung, by hand, every morning and night.

But our ability to connect with others ceased when we left the UK and were no longer speaking the same language as the locals. In my family, I'm the best with languages and the most outgoing, so it usually fell to me to attempt to communicate when we landed in a new place. But there were so many languages! Even with weeks of advance study, I barely spoke any of the seven languages I needed to use. Our lack of fluency made the connections with other people that had so delighted and comforted us nearly impossible. Until we got to Venice.

There, we took a ferry, then a water taxi, then walked the rest of the way to the snug Airbnb flat we'd rented. On the door was a little plaque, the name of the home: *Miracoli*. It was a word we immediately understood, no translation necessary: *Miracles*.

Our little rented flat got its name from the *Chiesa dei Miracoli*, Church of Miracles, which was just across from the apartment. The "Miracles" flat lived up to its name.

Miracoli was on the first floor of a deep blue, four-story building with flower boxes below every windowsill. Along the side of the flat, windows opened onto a canal. This canal, it turned out, was part of the gondoliers' typical loop through Venice. Our flat, on the ground floor, had windows just a few feet above the water level. Every day, we'd open those windows and sit in the sills, writing, drawing, praying, and watching Venice float gently by.

That's when the first small miracle happened. A gondolier stuck his tongue out at me. Just that. I smiled. He grinned back.

I began to smile at others when they caught my eye. Many smiled back. One asked for *caffè* (coffee) each time he passed, acting as if we were baristas and he was placing an order at our window. We laughed. We knew that word. But by the third pass, my girls began to worry that this gondolier was truly thirsty. It was hot, so they poured some cold juice from our tiny fridge into a cup and placed it on the sill. Then they kept their eyes peeled. The next time they saw him coming, they waved their arms and pointed with huge smiles to the drink on the windowsill. The gondolier immediately performed a rather incredible maneuver with his long pole to slide the boat close enough to receive his cup. The next time he passed us, he returned the empty cup and put his hand over his heart to express his appreciation.

On another day, the shutters on the kitchen window unexpectedly slammed shut. I'd never noticed a breeze in Venice and went to investigate. But before I made it, the shutters by the tiny kitchen table also snapped closed. Down the length of the flat, shutters were closing one at a time, in a slow line. Leah and I ran to the last window in time to see one of the gondoliers slide by with a smile. He had been closing the shutters, one by one, as he glided past—a joke! Community without words. *Miracoli* with its open windows helped us be close to people again, even without speaking the same language.

But this little place had an even deeper miracle in store.

One night, we decided to stroll through the streets of Venice. While the others finished getting ready, I went to wait outside. Venice looked so beautiful. Across the way, the Church of Miracles was lit with warm candle-light from within. I took a big breath of ocean air and ancient rock and let it out with delight.

As I did, an old Italian man made his way across the bridge that spanned the canal. He saw me breathe deep and smile. Seeing it, he stopped in front of me.

"*Sei Italiana?*" he asked.

I was surprised but managed to say "*no*" all the same. I am not Italian, but kind of honored to be mistaken for one.

"*Inglese?*" he guessed.

"*Sí.*" I replied.

That should have been the end of our conversation. I'd certainly reached the end of my Italian. But Italians have this endearing way of knowing you don't speak Italian and plowing right ahead as if you do. This old man just started talking to me in Italian, even after firmly establishing I couldn't speak his language. Not wishing to be rude, I listened and tried to keep up. I know Spanish, so every now and then I feel I'm close to under-standing a few words of Italian.

I heard the words eternal love (*amore eterno*) and tried to anticipate the punch line. "You are in the city of eternal love, *cara mia* . . . blah, blah, blah." I smiled and nodded gently.

But there was something I wasn't understanding because the old man wasn't leaving. He kept saying, with increasing emotion, "eternal love" while pointing to the church (not the canals or the gondolas).

And then he said a name I knew, even across the language barrier: *Gesù*.

Jesus.

He pointed. I followed his gnarled finger up the wall of the church. Sure enough, there was Jesus portrayed in beautiful marble relief, high up near the roof line.

There are passages in the Bible that talk about the gift of speaking in tongues and interpreting them. I have always believed these gifts help believers speak about Jesus across language barriers, just like at Pentecost. But I've never had those gifts. Not until that night, in the doorway of *Miracoli* apartment, when I suddenly understood what this Italian man had been trying so hard to tell me. He spoke again. It went something like this:

> Look at Jesus. Look at him.
> His hand is over his heart, like this (he models Jesus' pose in the marble relief).
> *That* means eternal love.
> On either side, two angels and two disciples.
> They all point at Jesus.
> Jesus points at his heart.
> He loves you with an eternal love.
> Eternal love for you.
> For *you*.
> Remember.
> *Ciao*.

As soon as the old Italian man saw that I really understood, he was gone.

Have you ever watched a good, steady rain hit thirsty ground? That's what the old man's words were to my heart. It was a miracle: to have someone reach out to tell me that God loves me. I had done nothing to deserve this man's kindness. On the contrary, I was clearly one of the thousands of foreign tourists that clogged up his city.

But he saw me sigh as I looked at the church. I'm not sure if he could tell if it was happy or sad. But he saw it, and he stopped. He wanted to make sure I knew that the Church of Miracles had a message of love for me. That *God* had a message of love for me.

God's love crosses borders of language and culture. Angels and disciples throughout time have pointed to Jesus, who points to his heart. A reminder, a call to remember that we are loved, eternally—whether we are at home or thousands of miles from all that is familiar.

Angels and disciples. I wondered for a while which the old man was— disciple or angel? And I was tempted to say angel, for what believer could be that brave?

I try for courage in my faith. I'm an introvert, but I push myself to talk to strangers on planes or soccer fields who want to know about Jesus. If they *ask*. Or if I can really tell they need me. But a stranger on the street who never asked? Oh my goodness, no.

I guess I have always assumed that if I talked to someone about Jesus without their permission, it might burden them. I know better now. The old man's words never felt like a burden, they have only ever been grace. For all the weeks that followed on my family's sabbatical, the old man's words were with me. When we hit a rough patch, or I was tired of learning new languages, or lonely, I'd remember that night in Venice, and what the old man said: eternal love, Jesus has that for you. It would immediately change my outlook. Years later, his words are with me still.

Angel or disciple? I'm not sure, but I think disciple. A believer in Venice stopped to tell a stranger of God's eternal love for her. Undaunted by the language barrier. Talking until she understood.

A gnarled finger pointing to Jesus' heart and then to mine.

You are loved, eternally.

Remember.

Ciao.

Could I be a disciple like that?
I'm not sure I'm brave enough.
But I want to be.

Could you be a disciple like that?
I'm not sure you're brave enough.
But I bet you want to be too.

Let's try, shall we? Because if we do try, if we speak of God's love, to strangers, across seemingly impossible barriers, and if just one of them feels the way I have ever since that day, it would be worth it.

It would be a miracle. Worked by an ordinary disciple. Like you. Like me.

Try This

- The next time you travel outside the US, assuming it's safe, get to know the local culture. Visit a restaurant where locals (not just tourists) eat, go to a community celebration or sporting event. Be a learner, polite and interested, teachable. Be ready to receive help, to feel childish and make mistakes. Give others a chance to be kind. Express your thanks.

- If you can't travel outside the US, cross cultures here. Try food from a different region of the world at a restaurant or food truck. Chat with the owner or staff. Visit a worship service outside your tradition. Most churches are happy to welcome guests. If you can, ask what's giving them life, what they are excited about, where God is breaking through. Folks love to share how God is moving among them.

Conclusion

Jesus taught in synagogues and on hillsides. He quoted Scripture, but also connected God's eternal message to daily objects: birds, farmers, housewives, and marketplaces. Jesus looked for God's work throughout the world and pointed it out to his followers. They saw God in common, everyday examples they could immediately understand. That creative, life-giving work of God hasn't stopped. God is still moving today throughout our world—in grocery stores, dance clubs, livestock auctions, and honky-tonk joints.

Perhaps, like me, you've always assumed that meeting God meant finding a quiet space, setting time aside, and separating yourself from daily life. These are wonderful ways to grow in faith, but they are not the only ways. We are busy, stressed, and anxious. Instead of only setting more time *aside* for God, let's give our attention to God *throughout* the days we are already living.

The early apostles expected to find evidence of God everywhere they went. Not just synagogues, but marketplaces (Acts 17:17), a meal with family, the beauty of a gentle rainstorm (both Acts 14:17), or the devastation of a shipwreck (Acts 27:21–26). Even foreign temples and statues to idols (Acts 17:22–23) became places where one might glimpse the Creator. It just took a faithful believer to see these moments as love letters from God and then "read" them to others.

Let's return to our searching roots. Let's hear God's call to a full-life faith. Let's expect to meet our Savior at work, in line, and in places that challenge and change us.

Across twenty years of ministry, I've taught myself to look at the world with hopeful eyes. To believe that God has beaten me to every single place I go and to seek out the evidence of God's love in that place. A trip to the town dump, a long wait at the bus stop, even the snarl of a Walmart parking lot, are places and opportunities to connect with the divine, to remind ourselves that God is already moving among us. More than ever, we need to embrace a spirituality that grows both in withdrawal *and* engagement.

Will you come with me? Will you join this journey?

Let's move through everyday life with the clear and joyful expectation of encountering God along the way. Jesus calls believers today to share good news in Jerusalem, Judea, Samaria, and then the ends of the earth (Acts 1:8). May you embrace a spirituality that is brave enough to believe God rules . . . everywhere.